T0327901

THEOREM[A]

THE BODY, EMOTION + POLITICS in FASHION

Filep Motwary

SKIRA

Interviews
Filep Motwary

Idea
Danilo Venturi

Management
Gianpaolo D'Amico

Production
Candice-Reney Jooste

Editorial coordination
Emma Cavazzini

Editing
Anna Albano

Graphic design
Open Lab

First published in Italy in 2018 by

Skira editore S.p.A.
Palazzo Casati Stampa
via Torino 61, 20123 Milano, Italy
www.skira.net

© 2018 Polimoda
© 2018 Filep Motwary for his texts
© 2018 Skira editore

Printed and bound in Italy. First edition

ISBN: 978-88-572-3913-2

Distributed in USA, Canada, Central & South
America by ARTBOOK | D.A.P. 75, Broad
Street Suite 630, New York, NY 10004, USA.
Distributed elsewhere in the world by Thames
and Hudson Ltd., 181A High Holborn, London
WC1V 7QX, United Kingdom.

CONTENTS

FOREWORD

Danilo Venturi

I have always considered myself to have an in-depth, chronologically ordered memory. Yet, when turning the lens to examine my own body and more specifically my mind, I struggle to remember exactly when I first met Filep Motwary. It had been as if I had always known him, as if he were my alter ego. In fact, every time we talk we never agree on anything but we always agree on what really matters in life. When it comes to Filep, what I do remember is how his interviews played a decisive part in the "Momenting The Memento" event, organised by Linda Loppa and inspired by my book of the same name. After the event and months of insisting, I managed to convince Filep to teach at Polimoda, as well as to start a series of interviews in order to write a new book.

What interested us was the direct testimony of human beings exactly as it is, and to place that at the centre of focus. There was no need to filter, copy and paste, quote, and pretend to be authors of philosophical macro-systems. It's the same approach that we use as educators. We can provide themes, models and tools, but in the end what we really want is that the personality of the students come out, eventually to the point of contradicting and amazing us. A book of interviews teaches us that there may be different languages, approaches and opinions on the same subject, although the interviewees all come from the creative industry. For me this is a small lesson of tolerance and an education to respect diversity.

If in "Momenting The Memento" we talked about Fetish, Monsters and Bridges, this time we wanted to focus on Body, Emotions and Politics. In the digital age the body experiences a great contradiction. Photoshop is the new cosmetic, the body is modified, and flaws are corrected, so the body is enhanced and somehow, augmented. On the contrary, our body is seen more in social networks than in the places where we find ourselves physically. The body here doesn't sweat, the image is flat, artificial and cold, so the body is somehow exposed but not lived, and therefore denied. And the paradox lies right in the fact that the more our image is swiped the more it is denied.

Moving from different premises we arrived at the same conclusion as Hussein Chalayan, when he showed that the more the dress gives way to nudity the less nudity is interesting, at the point that only a glance could give us back the emotion denied. What really matters is the space in between, that game called fashion that makes the difference between a helpless animal simply in need to cover itself to survive and the human being as an uncanny entity, evolved in all its splendour and ferocity. Reproduction and survival, Eros and Thanatos, are still the main engines of all our emotions, fears and wishes. Fashion is the stage where these engines are shown.

Each era has its dominant themes and fashion readily reflects them. The quest for a more sustainable world, the equality between genders as well as between people and freedom of expression, are what make us understand how the dressed body is a political statement in the same way as our actions. Fashion is entertaining, it helps us to live more lightly, it shouldn't be taken seriously. Nonetheless, fashion as a reflection of the society is also a privileged lens to see things more consciously. Perhaps that's why we insist on doing it, following it and commenting on it. Perhaps this is the reason why I wanted Filep Motwary to write this new book. The necessity to sharpen the focus on the interlinked trilogy of the body, the mind, and politics is what he has seamlessly managed to question in this provocative series of interviews.

Enjoy the reading.

PREFACE

Filep Motwary

THEOREM[A] as the title of this book, was chosen as a metaphor for fashion and its psycho-synthesis, based on the three terms "body, emotion and politics", as analysed by the pioneers, academics and designers contributing to this book, through interview testimonies.

These conversations were conducted either by phone, in person, Skype calls or email. My emphasis is on the body, collecting (perhaps) contrastive thoughts on its essence as well as how it is perceived; the vital element of emotion (as the key to longevity or poetic reality) and lastly the politics surrounding the current state of the fashion industry, as we (think we) know it.

The participants were selected for their professional integrity, their body of work and vast knowledge of historical and contemporary fashion, their gaze on fashion, and their contribution as a whole: Hussein Chalayan, Jean Paul Gaultier, Pamela Golbin, Iris van Herpen, Harold Koda, Michèle Lamy, Thierry-Maxime Loriot, Antonio Mancinelli, Suzy Menkes, Violeta Sanchez, Valerie Steele, Jun Takahashi from Undercover, Olivier Theyskens, Viktor & Rolf.

Lastly Nick Knight, whose interview is published solidly online on Polimoda.com

Throughout the process, I insist on certain questions, trying to gather individual views on similar matters.

INTERVIEWS

HUSSEIN CHALAYAN

Fashion Designer

BODY

FILEP MOTWARY: How relevant is the principle of covering the female body to conceal it from the male gaze today?

HUSSEIN CHALAYAN: This has to do with what context we are referring to, because every culture looks at this a bit differently. I think that all these issues about the male gaze are now in a way, an exploited subject, in the sense that it has a history. Now it is more about the human gaze, it is more about women looking at each other and not just men, it's about the gaze in general.

It's to do with what is missed out and what is covered; yet it is culture specific. In some cultures where the person is not seen as a sexual object, even if they are half naked, this is appearing not as vulgar whereas, in a culture where the person is sexualised it appears as something vulgar; it has to do with the actual environment that you are in.

If you look at Scandinavia and their idea of the body, it is obviously very different to the perception of the body in the Middle East. So I feel personally that it's very hard to talk about this without thinking which culture you apply this to and I think universal comments about how things should be are about our own ideals; universal opinions about this cannot apply to everybody.

Our own utopia for the body can't be forced upon other people, so it is very much about a "study" rather than having a very definite comment that you can apply to everyone. My utopia is about making new proposals, but I feel that we cannot really change the reality of various cultures.

FM: If you allow me to go back to your Spring 2003 show, where certain dresses appeared almost like entrails, like the silhouette was cut out in the front to see the intestines of the body, please correct me if I am wrong. What could be really fascinating about our organs?

HC: It was about disgust actually and I was looking at other parts of the body but at the end it may be perceived that way. It was my attempt to create something anatomical with the cut of the fabric and the twists. This is something that I had in other collections too but perhaps in less obvious ways.

I think it has to do with this; there is a reality of our bodies with its structure, the muscles, and the organs. When we are working on shapes on top of the body, if we are aware of what is underneath I think you draw differently and you start to look at lines and the silhouette from another perspective as well. So, I think I am interested in this relationship between understanding the body from outside to inside and then exploring the lines based on this. There is some kind of invisible relationship, if the drawn composition somehow relates to the body and your understanding of what is underneath, you can perhaps get better results.

FM: Do we really seek for a deeper meaning into clothing?

HC: This has to do more with an integrated approach to design where you understand structure and you extend it and relate to something else. I find that best design often comes when ideas are integrated with the body and to understand this you first need to understand the body well. It's a very hard thing to talk about; you need to be in practice as it is not an academically viable subject.

FM: According to Dr. Anthony Synnott's book "The Body Social" originally published in 1993, the transformations the body goes through in time also affect one's self and change it. How is the meaning of the "body" approached in fashion today, considering its permanent outline and the fact that it is something generic?

HC: It cannot be done in one way. We are living in an era where it's not about one approach anymore. In the past there was, for example the sixties approach, the seventies as well, you'd recognize it instantly. We are living in a very entitled era. The millennials are a very entitled generation, it's a really worrying moment. Social media has created this sense of knowledge that isn't experiential knowledge. This gives the notion that people know things just because they have access to data but you cannot learn by being exposed to information only — you learn from studying and applying. I think access to information is being used as a weapon of entitlement, not only with knowledge but also with a sense of having rights in many situations without earning those rights.

They are saying we have access to data therefore we know, therefore we feel!

Also we live in an era where you have despair and entitlement at the same time. Despair because many people whilst having rights are also suffering from feeling of missing out, especially in connection with the immediacy of social media, leading to a new hybrid of entitled but desperate individuals.

On the other hand I think that technology is the most exciting thing if it is used properly, it can create unimaginable scenarios as well as the democratisation of information. In some remote places you can connect to the Internet and you can have access to world knowledge, even if it's information which needs to be digested and not used only as data armour as discussed previously, in connection with data versus knowledge.

FM: Is there truly a way for the body to be trained in order to serve fashion?

HC: Yes, of course. There are codes of behaviour that allow the garment to be carried in a certain way. Perhaps this would happen more in the past rather than the present, women would be kind of prescribed codes of behaviour and how to move in the garment, how to walk. One good thing these days is that we have less rules, women are much more relaxed even in stiff evening attire, even wearing less make up, having more natural hair etc., it is the norm now.

FM: You are probably the pioneer who set the rules for the future of fashion with clothes that are actually transforming themselves on the body in an instant. What would be your prediction of the future body? The technological body, the one that is dressed by computerised clothing. Why does the body still need to look and act human?

HC: This is not even my opinion but we are obviously going to have much more integrated technology with the body, meaning that everything will get smaller and much more integrated with it. Let's bring to mind the first cell phones and how big they were compared to how they look now. We have chip technology that can be injected, and soon you will be able to use your hand as your travel card...

All of this is not even difficult to imagine. The body will soon be merged with even more things, even with language for example, we will be able to speak other languages perhaps based on chips that will be implanted into our skulls.

On the other hand we have people who are still very romantic about the past and might want to go backwards instead of forward as they will find this way more refreshing, which is the opposite extreme. Whilst many items of clothes will become much more functional as time passes, serving all kinds of purposes.

The future, I think, will also be about enhanced interaction with each other, possibly we will be in a place where we will be able to communicate without speaking. In a way I feel that technology will make the world even smaller than it is now, where connections which in my view are governed by our interests, will be even more the case diminishing identification based on nation states, or cultural affinity.

Meanwhile I feel that there will also be a romantic interest for ancient cultures, as a backlash to new technology in connection to nature, compassion and in the fields of health, diet, etc.

EMOTION

FM: How emotionally connected are you to the body you design for? Here I would like to refer to your Fall 2000 collection, the notion of the immigrant, the notion of belonging as well as our affiliation to the clothes we wear, our belongings in general.

HC: I can only answer this by my own perspective. Essentially I am an emotive designer, intellectualisation comes after. Something has to move me emotionally first. For me the collection you are referring to was much more about a result coming from personal experience and I thought about how I could turn a situation like that into a design exercise. That is why I also was posed questions to my family, etc. There is a sort or correlation between emotions and form and I always try to create my own language as to how I could translate that relationship.

For me it is about how to create a sense of life with design. If you create a narrative of working for yourself which is genuine and you really try to reflect emotions or the unseen, I believe you can create a better level of design. Using the invisible interests as a means to create form, but I do not know what to call this technique or how to explain it. I guess it has to do with synaesthesia and semiotics, if you look at it more deeply...

POLITICS

FM: **We witness how the modern fashion model's posture has changed, the use of hands, and the choreography for the most part, is now a rather straight walking line. How would you explain this phenomenon and the reasons behind these changes, if we compare it to twenty, thirty, forty years back?**

HC: It is a positive thing this change, it sexualise women less, even if misogyny and sexism still exist. I would like to think that we are living in a post-feminist environment, however unfortunately women are still not entirely empowered, there is a long way to go still, but I am hopeful for the future.

JEAN PAUL GAULTIER

Couturier

BODY

FILEP MOTWARY: How connected are you to the body you design for?

JEAN PAUL GAULTIER: Very. I do sketches of course, but I work a lot more during the fittings on the body. However, my designs can be later interpreted for different shapes. I am not fixated on one body type. I find beauty everywhere and most of all in difference.

FM: How connected is society to the clothes they choose to wear? Do we seek for a deeper meaning into clothing?

JPG: Designers are a reflection of their times. We respond to the world around us and we need to show the changes in the society. When I designed the skirt for men, I did it because I saw that people around me were ready for it. One of my models, Stéphane Sednaoui, now a famous photographer, returned from Bali wearing a sarong. It was one of many things that showed me that I could show the skirt for men.

Clothing has meaning as it can help us give a message, make a statement, or hide and pretend to be someone else.

FM: Your work does not only serve in dressing the body, you are a pioneer in reforming and reshaping it. Why this particular need?

JPG: I suppose that you mean the corset. Instead of being an instrument of submission for me it has always been an instrument of liberation. Women can choose to be seductive on their own terms.

My grandmother told me that in the old days women would drink a glass of vinegar and when their stomach would contract that was when the corset would be tightened. There was a certain expectation for women to have a certain body shape.

Nowadays you can choose to wear a corset but it would be your choice, not the choice of the society.

FM: You initially started as a prêt-à-porter designer, then added menswear followed by Haute Couture to eventually keep the last as the one that interests you the most. Could you share with me the main reasons of this choice and what Haute Couture served then, compared to now?

JPG: The world of the prêt-à-porter has changed beyond recognition for me. I had started in the couture in 1970 at Pierre Cardin and continued at Jacques Esterel and Jean Patou, but I soon felt that fashion was happening elsewhere, in the ready-to-wear. I started my fashion house with nothing; I jumped and learned to swim later. In the eighties the real creativity was concentrated in the ready-to-wear and some of the things that I or other designers like Claude Montana or Thierry Mugler or Azzedine Alaïa did were almost like couture. My corset dress from 1982 needed to be made by hand like a couture dress.

But after almost forty years of doing the ready-to-wear I felt it was time for me to stop. At the time I started there were no big groups, one could thrive based on the creativity and passion alone.

Haute couture allows me to stay in fashion and continue to experiment while giving me the opportunity to work on other projects like the show that I am preparing for 2018, called Fashion Freak Show. It will be presented at the Folies-Bergère from October 2018.

FM: Today we experience a shift in the way the body is represented in general fashion, as well as through imagery. The previous decades were overly sexual, thus today the body is almost fully covered. Why in your opinion?

JPG: I have felt acutely for the past decade a big return of conservatism. I would never have been able to do today what I did in the eighties. We are paradoxically freer in some areas but in many others the society is more conservative and politically correct.

FM: Historically speaking, how did the silhouettes get defined compared to the current state of the silhouette?

JPG: There was a certain expectation from the society on the body shape. Also there was a time where men's clothes were even more extravagant than women's. It's only the nineteenth century that took away the colour and made the black suit a men's uniform in the West.

FM: How is the meaning of the "body" approached in fashion, considering its permanent outline and the fact that it is something generic?

JPG: Without body there is no fashion. It is generic but at the same time each body is different. It's like snowflakes. No two are alike.

EMOTION

FM: How can you manoeuvre emotion through your work?

JPG: I hope that it is obvious that I do my job with passion. If I had no passion anymore I would have stopped doing fashion.

FM: I will never forget your 1994 Spring Summer collection and what a great impact it had on me as a teenager as well as on the whole society. Why is the ceremonial process of dressing linked with achieving a higher state of feelings?

JPG: That is one collection that I am very proud of. Tattoos at the time were not as ubiquitous as now and I felt that the collection had a big impact. I had gone to a tattoo congress in the UK and seen amazing things. I was so taken over by the beauty that I decided to make a whole collection based on tattoos. I don't know if clothes take us to a higher spiritual level, at least in our Western culture, but as I said the clothes and the skin are very important for self-expression.

FM: In your experience as a designer who is known for applying history into contemporary clothing; how does history serve the feature based on your perspective and approach?

JPG: Of course I have had historical inspirations but I do not like to take them literally. I prefer to make an interpretation that is much more modern.

FM: Could we suggest clothing is a living organism?

JPG: Because in the end it dies. Every piece of clothing has a certain lifespan and when it comes to an end it is retired like us — sometimes buried, sometimes burned...

FM: Your exhibition is a world-renowned phenomenon. I wonder if you are interested to observe people visiting to see your "stories"? Would you be interested to examine their psycho-synthesis and perhaps question the reasons their interest is stimulated by your work? Why, how would it serve you?

JPG: I did this job to be loved. The biggest compliment for me is to see someone wearing my designs on the street. So yes, of course I am interested in what people think about my clothes but at the same time I always did what I wanted without thinking of marketing, or of what is "fashionable". As they say, "la mode se démode". So yes, in a way it would be the ultimate flattery to listen to what people like about my work but at the same time it wouldn't serve me much as I always did what I felt was important, not what others tried to impose on me.

FM: At which point fashion makes us feel vulnerable?

JPG: If we follow it too much. When you become a slave to fashion it makes you vulnerable.

POLITICS

FM: How does the media serve you and how do you serve the media?

JPG: My generation of designers was the first that was recognised by the wider public. Before, in the sixties and seventies, we didn't know what the designers looked like. Maybe we would see them for two minutes on TV twice a year during the couture shows.

For better or for worse, Claude Montana, Thierry Mugler, Azzedine Alaïa, and myself, we started being photographed and interviewed. MTV came, fashion programs came, and now on the social networks we can see everything that is happening more or less in real time.

I have always loved different challenges, so I presented Eurotrash with Antoine De Caunes, I was once a presenter for the MTV Music Awards with ten costume changes... But I did all that to have fun, not as a conscious decision to be in the media.

FM: How is fashion revelatory of the social mechanism and politics?

JPG: As I said, designers have to feel "l'air du temps". They have to react to the society and the changes in the society; otherwise we are not doing our job.

FM: Why do "body standards" change over the years while certain attributes remain as classics? What are the JPG classics in the anatomy of the way you dress the body?

JPG: Maybe you think of my codes: masculine/feminine and androgyny, corset, navy stripes.

FM: Not more than twenty years ago, certain designers (like you, McQueen, John Galliano) were creating entire collections inspired by tribes, global historical references and folklore. Today this approach is considered as inappropriate. What happened in between?

JPG: I would say at the risk of sounding reactionary that the political correctness happened. There was no talk of cultural appropriation at the time. I have always had the utmost respect for different cultures and always tried to show that keeping one's own traditions was important and that there is beauty in difference.

That is what I wanted to show with my Chic Rabbi collection. I saw once a group of Orthodox Jews on the steps of the New York library and I was struck by the beauty of their attire and the fact that they kept up their traditions. I found that incredibly beautiful and used it as inspiration for a collection.

FM: What about the modern tribes formed by our affiliation to a certain designer?

JPG: Tribes will always exist, we had punks, we had neo-romantics, in the seventies and eighties we had skaters and surfers and now we have kids that are nostalgic for the times that they didn't know.

FM: How does designing fashion help you/us understand society? What are the needs covered through fashion?

JPG: We all have to dress, we all have to wear clothes and we all say something through the clothes, and I don't mean by wearing expensive designer clothes. By looking at a photo we can guess the decade by just looking at the clothes. So clothes are here not just to keep us warm but for self-expression as well.

PAMELA GOLBIN

Chief Curator of Fashion and Textiles
at the Musée des Arts Décoratifs, Paris

BODY

FILEP MOTWARY: How connected are fashion designers to the body they design for today?

PAMELA GOLBIN: You may loosely place designers into two categories; those who start their creative process by draping on the body and those who begin by sketching. Madeleine Vionnet and Cristóbal Balenciaga are examples of couturiers that would create their silhouettes through a draping process. Christian Dior or Yves Saint Laurent would first sketch hundreds of silhouettes at the start of their collections.

More recently, a designer such as Azzedine Alaïa based all of his work directly on the female figure cutting, pinning, pleating on his fit model's body. More conceptual and narrative, the Cypriot Hussein Chalayan is particularly interested in telling a personal story where the female body comes in after his narrative is set. Some designers both sketch and drape. It hinges not only on the designer's rapport with the body but also on their personal creative process as well as their training. Depending on their affinities or otherwise with the female form, they will have a very different approach to designing.

FM: Before we started recording this conversation, you said something very interesting, there are designers who are afraid of the body and they don't want to see it… Why then someone chooses to become a designer if not for praising the body?

PG: The body is not always central to the work of every designer. It greatly depends on what their interests are and why they choose fashion to express themselves. In the sixties, Paco Rabanne, for example, was particularly interested in using new materials such as aluminium plates and introducing different ways of construction. During the same period, Pierre Cardin put forth a new business model in fashion where licensing and signature style came together. Neither of these points of view were centred around the female body — they were rather more disruptive ways of looking at production and design.

It is interesting to note that Christian Dior, the iconic couturier who in 1947 introduced the "New Look", always kept a distance from the female body. Not only did he begin his collections by using pencil and paper but as the photos chronicle he often used a long stick to point out corrections to be made, without touching his models or the prototype dress. And thus, creating a distance between the body, the woman and himself. Even if Dior had a less hands-on approach to the female form he did design and define one of the most important feminine shapes of the twentieth century.

FM: Christian Dior's "Corolle", or "New Look" collection as Carmel Snow baptised it, brought back abandoned forming body methods like the corset. Why do you think it had so much effect then that we still see it in contemporary fashion?

PG: Christian Dior's "New Look" will exemplify the modern definition of femininity. He grew up during La Belle Époque, at a time when a women's hourglass figure was the defining factor of her beauty. It was a moment where corsetry was extremely important in constructing and shaping the figure and more symbolically the notion of femininity. Dior's aesthetic was certainly informed by his personal cultural landscape. It is not by chance that his "New Look" silhouette was based on soft shoulders and a cinched waist reminiscent of his childhood memories and in direct reaction to the masculine shapes prevalent during the wartime years. The "New Look" becomes the expression of an entire era. Each fashion designer presents his own interpretation of this style, which is the archetype of propriety. In order to construct his silhouette, Dior reshaped the female body with girdles and revived an entire industry that had suffered during the war.

Fashion is often about extremes; from spectacularly corseted silhouettes that exude a form of femininity to particularly masculine or androgynous forms that question sexuality.

FM: Why is the corset a sign of authority onto the body? Why is the oppression of the body always present in fashion, ever since Dior re-launched it? A sort of fetishism...

PG: To wear a corset in the late nineteenth century was a long-term commitment that began when one was a toddler and shaped and transformed a woman's body throughout her life. The hyper-feminine body was not only visibly restrained from the outside but all of the internal organs were just as equally repositioned, which is why women would wear their corsets up to 23 hours a day.

Today, new stretch materials give a corseted look to the silhouette without oppressing it. It can be an integral part of the dress or simply used as an accessory that is no longer part of a ritual that was imposed on every woman's life throughout the second half of the nineteenth century and the beginning of the twentieth. So it has changed dramatically. That being said, some of today's high-heeled shoes are just as challenging to wear as corsets from the past.

You could argue that having mastery over one's life and destiny is a modern goal for many. Diets, sports and exercise in general allows us to have some control over our own body, even if it is only fleeting.

FM: Do we seek for a deeper meaning into clothing? Can fashion be didactic? If so, at what level?

PG: For me, fashion is one of the most powerful tools that we have to express something about ourselves. A visual language with complex rules and a sophisticated vocabulary, fashion allows us to present a facet of who we are. Whether you make a conscious choice or not, what you select to wear every morning delivers a message to those who see you. It is a non-verbal language but extremely influential.

FM: We have been desperately exploring or trying to re-define the silhouette for centuries now. Humans have been working on reconstructing the body and proportion through clothing... Why this particular need?

PG: Change comes from appropriating an object and being able to then imagine it differently. Within the fashion realm, to be able to appropriate the body means that you are not only defining but understanding what your body is about. Without that understanding you can't move forward and change it. It's a way of learning in the end, quite simply. What is the body about? This is the first question you ask in order to understand it and then change it. Nicolas Ghesquière mentioned, "Never forget that what has become timeless was once really new." Fashion is always about the newness of the past that is brought up to speed in the present.

EMOTION

FM: How can we manoeuvre emotion through fashion?

PG: I think both are so entwined, that you cannot have one without the other and that's probably one of fashion's greatest attributes and also its biggest challenge. A piece of cloth is charged not only with one's own emotion but also that of the person who sees you in it and the designer who actually made it. Creativity is essentially all about emotion.

FM: I wonder at which point fashion makes us feel vulnerable?

PG: When something has so much power, it can be overwhelming as well and for some it can be very confusing. The fear of "missing out" is definitely part of the fashion system, where not having the "it" bag, the "it" garment, the "it" object, and consequently not being part of the "it" crowd is always quietly present in the background.

FM: In your experience as an academic, putting together so many wonderful exhibitions, catalogues and outstanding projects... I wonder if you were interested in observing people visiting your "stories".

PG: Every project is a fresh start and I have to approach it with an open mind, free of any preconceived ideas I may have on the designer or theme. But it's always a collaborative process. In all of my projects, my aim is always to create dialogues, a triangular conversation between the designers, the exhibition visitors and myself. A dialogue that is inclusive, where emotion and inspiration come together to tell part of the story.

Whether living or not, my job is to define the signature style of a designer, highlight what makes them different, and showcase the signature visual aesthetic, proper to their values, in a way that draws in and stimulates a modern audience.

FM: What is so important about being new? Does creation have to be new?

PG: There is a wonderful quote by Alexander McQueen. "The new doesn't exist. Even in the most contemporary design. Nothing is new under the sun. Materials evolve, fabrics change [...] But, even if themes are different, everything is part of the same whole."

At the same time, the "new" changes the context of the "old" and allows us to see things from another perspective.

POLITICS

FM: How would you describe the approach of all the designers that took over the house of Dior through the years, from Yves Saint Laurent, to Marc Bohan, Gianfranco Ferré, John Galliano, Raf Simons, Maria Grazia Chiuri? What are the differences and similarities and what are the politics, if any, behind the way they approached Dior's vision?

PG: I would begin by saying that what is extraordinary about the House of Dior is that its founder, Christian Dior, established his name worldwide in only ten years. In a mere decade, he was able to establish the aesthetic and commercial blue print of the House that is still relevant and modern today. The fashion designers who continued and expanded on Dior's vision, reflected the fashion landscape of their times. Yves Saint Laurent had a short tenure but brought the youthful vision of a 21 year old. He arrived on the scene as a precursor of the youthquake that would blossom in the sixties. Marc Bohan takes the reins of the House as of 1960 and designs elegant fashions for crowned princesses and socialites during the next three decades. The arrival of Gianfranco Ferré as of 1987 reflects the recognition and importance of Italian fashion, which had gone through a transformation from its early days in the fifties in Florence. By the eighties, Milan was the epicentre of fashion in Italy and Ferré's arrival at Dior signalled the importance Italian fashion had taken.

And then of course, in 1997, you have the arrival of John Galliano. He was part of an Anglo-Saxon wave that swept through many Parisian houses. Alexander McQueen took over Givenchy, the American Marc Jacobs took the artistic direction of Louis Vuitton, Michael Kors settled into Céline and Narciso Rodriguez was appointed at Loewe. John Galliano's fifteen-year collaboration brought incredible critical acclaim and financial success to the house.

The Belgian designer Raf Simons followed for three years introducing a more minimalist approach to Dior's feminine vocabulary. Most recently, Maria Grazia Chiuri, the first woman designer to work as creative director, was named to the venerable house.

FM: How is fashion revelatory of the social mechanism and politics?

PG: Amazingly so! You have the speechwriter and you have the wardrobe maker of every politician. You have the spoken word and you have the visual word, they go together and you cannot have one without the other. It's out of question in today's world where images are almost superseding the words.

FM: What about the way it is formed today? Who is directing it?

PG: In the fashion industry what has truly changed is its scale and the sophistication. Back in the eighteenth century the visual language of fashion was extremely important. Just as a military uniform, civil dress allowed you to place the wearer within a cultural, political and economic context visually understanding the social rank of the person with whom you were interacting in order to engage with that person in conventional confines.

Today that still exists but what has changed is that the finesse of the industry allows small, niche groups to express "who I am and what I stand for" within the social order of that small group. For example you have the rappers, you have the goths, you have the skaters or the surfers, and each have their own specific wardrobe with multiple brands that cater to them following their own pre-established rules.

Urban and active wear are now part of more generalised offer. What was once niche has become available to a much larger audience. The scale is now global whereas before it was very local.

FM: Is there any sort of hierarchy in fashion as you see it?

PG: Like in many other industries, price naturally sets up a hierarchy. Structurally, the apex of the fashion system is the Parisian Haute Couture followed by the prêt-à-porter, the contemporary mass market and the fast fashion market.

Creatively, however, there is less and less of a hierarchy because of a more direct access between designers and their clients.

FM: Would you agree that fashion now, more than ever before, has become self-referential, much more closed and entirely for those who are following fashion? Some designers use the terms "family" or "tribe", so we have the Givenchy, the Balmain and the Rick Owens tribes and so on...

PG: You are very right to bring this forward. Today can be a challenging moment for many people because of globalisation and the myriad of choices that it has brought. Until recently, big cities brought together several million people, now they are populated with up to 20 million people. When you are faced with such a great number, you want to find a way to make things more personal so that you don't feel that you have disappeared within such a large group.

It is very important to keep those tribal or more local aspects active so that you can appropriate the language. It's as if each territory adds its specific accent, a certain originality within the confines of a larger picture. Being part of a more intimate circle gives you a certain sense of security as well as the sentiment of belonging. Wearing the clothes of that group allows you to share and display the same values. It's about making your own life more relevant on a local level when everything has gone global.

FM: How are myths in fashion getting developed around certain subjects or people? How does fantasy serve reality? Should it, in contemporary culture? Is there room for nuance, fantasy, and extravagance?

PG: There is always room for nuance, fantasy and extravagance! It just so happens that there are moments in history when it's more prevalent than others.

FM: Why in your opinion matters that have been solved already are rising to the surface again? Focusing on fashion, designers are being judged today for their resources of inspiration? What happened in between?

PG: What is the role of the designer today? In the eighties and nineties, fashion — once the exclusive domain of a handful of international capitals — became a truly global industry, forcing the new generation of designers to evolve in order to meet the demands of the market. Creative talent was no longer the only criterion sought by the mega-brands that held sway. Fashion designers were required to be even more efficient in terms of marketing and artistic direction while taking on the role of spokesperson of the brand. The talented stylist is now an iconic figure, a multidisciplinary genius, both ambassador, spokesperson and master of ceremonies. And the fashion spectacle continues to beguile season after season, year after year to an ever-increasing global acclaim.

IRIS VAN HERPEN

Fashion Designer

BODY

FILEP MOTWARY: How connected are you to the body you design for?

IRIS VAN HERPEN: The body is my canvas and she is my continuous source of inspiration. As a former dancer I learned to look at what is there (to the body) as much as what is not there, I learned how transformable the body is and discovered how she relates (or sometimes not) to the space around her. I started shaping patterns that dissimulate the body's perspective or sometimes even subtract it.

FM: How connected is society to the clothes they choose to wear? Do we seek for a deeper meaning into clothing?

IVH: To me clothes can touch that deeper layer, having the power to change you emotionally and the right clothes can give you the power to communicate with people around you on a deeper level, an unconscious level, like smell can do.

Wearing something exceptionally beautiful that is made with lots of thoughts and lots of care is like listening to a beautiful piece of music that overwhelms you. Fashion to me is linked to a deep expression of desire, mood, cultural setting and personal expression.

FM: Should our physical structure and body outline serve an important factor to the decision whether we should follow fashion or not?

IVH: No one should follow fashion... Daring to discover your own style is much more powerful than to follow a mass (commercially driven) guide, being able to actually express your moods, your thoughts... daring to be creative in that.

I have grown into being a woman and this feeling of femininity is leading me much more than ever before, I dare to use my intuition now. It changed my approach to what fashion should be, I consider what is not there as much as what is (same when I look at the body), and that transformative power gives me freedom.

Today I take fashion as a moving entity. Much of the things I've learned about it I have let go, I need that space for disruption and intuition.

FM: Your work somehow suggests clothing is a living organism? A fantastic example is your Bird Dress from Fall 2013 Haute Couture collection. Could this reference be used as a prophecy of what is to come?

IVH: To me the Bird Dress connects to something very big and very small at the same time. It was wilderness embodied, expressing the powerful forces of nature, chaos and the magnetism between attraction and repulsion. Those are the big forces it expresses to me, the Bird Dress is also an expression of me when I was little. A young bird, a small black crow fell from our chimney, disowned from its parents. So we raised it, taught it to fly, and became very good friends, it would even wait for me outside on a tree of my primary school for my lunch breaks. The Bird Dress, I made it for this bird, to those memories of an unusual friendship, visualising this surreal and beautiful (and important) languages between man and nature. The world will change in ways we cannot even imagine today, I see collaboration as core to the future of fashion, shaping it into new realities.

FM: And what does Iris van Herpen clothing serve?

IVH: Each garment and every collection is a research into new understanding and discovery, on the conceptual level, on the level of materiality, on the level of techniques (in and outside of fashion) and on the level of beauty.

To me art, including fashion, is the engine of a society, it's the heart of what we see and how we think, it's freedom.

FM: Your computational approach, generating forms through a specific process on a screen... How do you define the outcome? When does the body come into the process?

IVH: Eight years ago, when I was working on my first 3D-printed dress, we would digitally draw it in three dimensions, working on a 3D-modelled virtual model.

After the dress came out of the 3D printer, I would see it on a real person for the first time. For the rest of the collection, I would be working on handmade garments, where I would drape the materials on a mannequin and then hand develop and hand stitch all the textures into dresses.

So the computational process and the hand-worked processes were living next to each other. But I changed this separation soon after, I started to mix the processes of the hand and the digital. I will give you one example of how a dress is created (every dress has a different process so this is only one example out of many). When I see or think of a texture that inspires me (this can come from nature, a detail in architecture, the work of an artist, etc.) either I will try to explain this to my team or show them. A drawing/sketch is done by hand (either by me or my team), then based on that sketch another drawing is made digitally. I choose the right material that we then laser-cut to the file we drew.

Then we heat press, hand stitch or machine stitch the laser-cut textures onto an "under" dress. Mostly a first sample isn't right yet. So the alteration rounds start — this can be five or ten times of adjustments and changes, it's always different. When the texture is exactly right, we will make bigger samples that I can drape directly on the mannequin in my studio. This takes several hours up to several days of draping; it is a very intuitive process between the "body" and my hands only. In this process I don't want to think too much, it's right when I feel it's right. This is the closest state of meditation I can be in.

When the drape is done, the pattern making starts, which is handwork again. When the patterns are finished, they are digitalised, so the textures can be adjusted very precisely to the patterns of the body that I draped. Then we have our final digitalised textures, made to measure. Then the process of making the final garment starts — this can be done fully by hand, sometimes partly 3D printed, laser cut, 3D moulded, magnetically "grown", etc. From this description, you can see that all the processes are so mixed; there is not any difference for me anymore if I draw something quickly by hand or on the computer. All tools are equal to me. What is essential to me is that the design is done physically on a mannequin or a real person, so I can see the movement in real life and I can feel the textures.

FM: We have been desperately exploring or trying to re-define the silhouette for centuries now. Humans have been working on reconstructing the body and proportion through clothing... Why this particular need?

IVH: That is a big philosophical question and it's the same question and answer to why it is we are reconstructing our world, our everything, and ourselves... If I speak from my own search for transformation, one of the most influential things in my life has been my classical ballet practice. During those years of dance I learned so much about my body, the power between mind and body, the transformation of movement, the "evolution" of shape, and more precisely how I could manipulate both shape and movement. Those years of dancing were the ground of my interest in fashion. I don't think I would have become a fashion designer if I hadn't danced. Now I feel able to transform this kinaesthetic knowledge into new shapes and materiality. If we look at life, at nature, at evolution... everything changes. Changing ourselves is about finding new forms of beauty, and seduction, and in the end about getting to know us better.

Fashion can give us a new space to move our thoughts around in an unfamiliar space in which to imagine. Through my work, I try to reach beyond our usual understanding of physical reality.

EMOTION

FM: How can you manoeuvre emotion through your work?

IVH: Often a material inspires me to start designing, the technique comes after. Mostly my design process starts out very "controlled" with an idea that comes from logic. And then after seeing a first test, a new idea comes, and the adjustment process starts, and that can go forward and backward hundreds of times — and along that intense and emotional path of trial and error all logic becomes chaos. And that moment of surrender to the chaos is where to me the most intense beauty is found, where intuition and emotion is at its most powerful. And this you can see in the outcome, the garment, that more than a human hand has shaped it. There is a natural beauty to be found in it.

FM: Why is the ceremonial process of dressing linked with achieving a higher state of feelings?

IVH: The start of the ceremony is the act of choosing. We create ourselves and our wellbeing through our taste and interests, we choose the music we like, the books we read, the films we watch, the places we go to, the art we look at, the clothes we wear. All that together is your identity that is created by you.

The more carefully you choose, the better you know what you want, the more this will enrich you. Wearing a particular garment that really expresses how I feel at that moment gives me a lot of comfort, it enables me to focus on the things that matter, it's like it encourages my awareness.

FM: In your experience as a designer whom is known for applying the "future" into clothing — I wonder if you are interested in observing people visiting galleries or museums to see your "stories" and examine their psycho-synthesis and perhaps question the reasons their interest is stimulated by your work?

IVH: Logically I would answer yes, but the answer is no to be honest. And this is because my process is one that comes from intuition. I don't want to lose that by analysing. My intelligence/brains are very essential to sorting out construction, innovation, and complex craftsmanship, but when it comes to design, it's my hands deciding. If I design from thinking only, it doesn't satisfy me. It doesn't give me that transformative power of making the unthinkable. So I leave my design process to my unconscious, my heart and my guts basically.

FM: At which point fashion makes us feel vulnerable?

IVH: For a lot of people fashion — the way they dress — tells their story, who they are, their interests, their values, perhaps even their role in society. The clothes people wear can be a very personal expression of their identity — when this isn't accepted by some people, or the society they live in, this can make a person very vulnerable.

FM: How do you reflect [emotional] tension in some of your garments? How is this achieved metaphorically and literally? I'm thinking of the Water Dress from Fall Winter 2012 Haute Couture collection.

IVH: My collections are small, so I can make every garment I design a very personal expression of how I feel and what I think at that moment. They are like time capsules. Every dress opens up a little diary of memories to me.

Some dresses are the beginning of a friendship, or even a new way of thinking.

Like the Skeleton Dress, that expresses my feelings of my body while parachute jumping, where there is not above or under, nor inside or outside. The Skeleton Dress represents freedom and imperfection to me, and between those two is where new perspectives can be found. The Water Dress represents metamorphosis and fragility. It reveals and encapsulates at the same time the body wearing it. It stills a fraction of time and movement, while stretching nature's behaviours and pattern making infinitely.

FM: Where does science and emotion meet? How do you think/work in achieving this goal?

IVH: In my first years I was focused on handwork and craftsmanship only (I didn't even use a sewing machine). Now my process has become much more collaborative, interacting with architects, scientists and engineers to create garments that combine experimental technology with traditional craftsmanship.

My work embodies exactly the opposite of what generally fashion is today. I go back to forgotten craftsmanship and the love for the handwork and at the same time I'm embedding new technologies and multidisciplinary collaborations. I intentionally stretch the edges of my medium, and some collaborations take me out of my own bubble of knowledge and experience, creating a kind of collective intelligence. This interdisciplinary research creates a constant dialogue and new knowledge.

The interaction between precision and serendipity, the artificial and the organic, the human touch and the might of machines captures duality, which is at the core of everything I make. I think this type of collaboration, and the sharing among specialists in diverse disciplines, is the future of fashion. They'll advance fashion in ways previously unimaginable. And that unimaginable new world of fashion is what keeps me exploring.

POLITICS

FM: Is there any sort of hierarchy in fashion as you see it? Who is directing it?

IVH: I don't really see fashion as a pyramid. There are all these systems within systems within systems. It's quaquaversal... people's powers are spreading in different directions all at the same time, like a CEO has the power on what direction a brand is going the years he/she is on board, at the same time bottom up the new generation of designers and graduates are working on the future direction of fashion, its long-term powers interfering with short-term powers and all influencers in between. So to speak of a few people deciding everything, that's a myth.

FM: What forces these changes in your opinion? From "The Birth of Venus" (c. 1486) by Botticelli, to Marie Antoinette, Louise Brooks, Bettie Page, Twiggy, Kim Kardashian...

IVH: It's the continuous dialogue between the arts and society, this continuous loop between reality and fantasy. What I see today is very positive; we see very different body proportions as being our example, our icons. It's not this one ideal projection of a woman anymore. Because both models and celebrities are our covers and the ones we adore, all kind of proportions and femininity is shown. This is much more varied than history has ever seen before.

FM: How are myths in fashion getting developed around certain subjects or people? How does fantasy serve reality? Should it, in contemporary culture? Is there room for nuance?

IVH: I don't think there are myths in fashion. Fashion is a myth. It's built on myths, there is no separation between the creation, the story telling, the sales, people falling in love, the buying and the wearing. Myths have created collective beliefs, dreams and hopes in the past, and modern myths do the same today, a lot more than we realise.

FM: Not more than twenty years ago, designers such as McQueen and John Galliano were creating entire collections inspired by tribes, global historical references and folklore. Today this approach is considered inappropriate. What happened in between?

IVH: I am not sure if I have a answer to this, but I think it's the mass communication that has made "a meaning" rather sensitive. Intentions are judged globally and in seconds only, losing all depth of meanings. A concept, a vision, an intention developed over months is translated and flattened towards simple one-liners, rapidly twisted and then easily projected onto existing frustrations in society.

FM: In your opinion does the longevity of these contemporary fashion "tribes" depend on the creative timeline of the designer's relevancy or will it be infinite?

IVH: It's working both ways, a good designer inspires his or her "tribe", creating and adding relevancy. At the same time there is always a time's vision that is influenced by trillion things, that are out of the hands of a designer. So infinity or a long relevance depends also on the footprint that a designer places within the time's vision.

FM: At what level are we conscious of what we see, buy, or wear? Does it matter?

IVH: We are able to see what we buy and wear, but not everyone wants to see it. We can be conscious about it, but not everyone wants to be. Luckily more and more people are opening up their eyes, becoming more conscious consumers, influencing the makers. It matters a huge deal, as fashion is one of the most pollutive industries to our planet. Both the consumer and the makers hold the power to decide if this will change or not. As a designer I am developing materials and techniques to help improve sustainability, and as a consumer I am conscious about what I buy and also buying less, realising I only need a few good pieces, not many of poor quality. Certainly we cannot continue making and buying like we do today, so "choose" is the key word for our future.

HAROLD KODA

Author and former Curator in Charge at the Costume
Institute of the Metropolitan Museum of Art, NYC

BODY

FILEP MOTWARY: How connected are fashion designers today to the body they design for?

HAROLD KODA: All apparel is necessarily a formal response to the body it clothes. Contemporary designers for the most part conform to the pragmatics of taking fabric and draping or tailoring it to the body utilising techniques that have evolved over time. However, there are a handful of designers who approach their work from a more conceptual perspective, or utilise unprecedented technologies, in their address of the body. This can lead to effects that can exaggerate aspects of the anatomy or eradicate any sense of the body at all. In the end though, the body supports the design so it is always referenced or, in some unusual examples, repudiated.

FM: How connected is society to the clothes they choose to wear? Do we seek for a deeper meaning into clothing?

HK: Clothing is so connected to issues of class, gender, group identity, individual expression that it cannot be separated from a societal manifestation. Clothing is a communication of who we are in the context of others. It truly doesn't matter what you wear in solitude, but as soon as you go into a situation with other people, what you are wearing situates and identifies you in ways that are implicit and explicit. Dressing might be seen as a personal consideration, but in its full functioning it is a social act.

FM: Should our physical structure and body outline serve an important factor to the decision whether we should follow fashion or not?

HK: I wouldn't advocate that categorically. It is more important to dress your concept of yourself. Clothing speaks to who you are or how you wish to be seen. Each of us should strive to give as articulate a presentation of ourselves as possible. The only bad fashion mistake is to project something you do not intend to project, to have what you wear misrepresent you.

FM: Mr Koda, in what ways could we suggest that clothing is a living organism?

HK: Fashion might be seen as an organic system, simultaneously alive and growing with parts withering and dying. Clothing is simply its material manifestation. Apparel is the material evidence of a phase in the fashion system, momentary and evolving.

FM: What does clothing serve today?

HK: Clothing always speaks to who we are as individuals and as a society.

FM: Being Harold Koda, how would you say exhibiting fashion serves in understanding the body? What about our society?

HK: Costume and fashion exhibitions today approach the subject from so many different perspectives: social history, aesthetic theory, gender studies, ethnography, political history, etc.

Almost twenty years ago, I did a purely formalistic survey of the manipulation of the body through dress. By avoiding any address of the history of fashion, of cultures and societies that produced the clothes (one could legitimately question this methodology), I sought to establish whether there are any ideals of the body that are in the human DNA, an evolutionary imperative. What I found was that fat, thin, long-waisted, short-waisted, big-bosomed, small-bosomed, ample buttocks, no buttocks, long feet, short feet, any zone of the body, appeared at some time or in some place to be seen as ideal and in repudiation of other times and places. There are studies that suggest that healthy hair, clear skin, good teeth, muscular symmetry (the attributes in my mind of a beautiful horse) are evolutionarily ordained physical ideals, but in terms of the cultural imposition of apparel on the body, all the rules are tossed.

FM: Historically speaking, how did the silhouettes get defined compared to the current state of the silhouette?

HK: I've always thought, but it is unsubstantiated by any studies, at least that I could find, that there is simply the fatigue of habit that generates fashionable change. When something becomes familiar, we tend to cease to experience it. Perhaps the human psyche craves an incremental novelty. The most interesting part for me is that in casting off one established aesthetic, something considered unattractive or ugly can be accepted and embraced.

FM: Why do body standards change over the years while certain attributes remain as classics?

HK: In a famine, a voluptuous body will seem enviable. In a world of plenitude, someone heavy might appear self-indulgent, even gluttonous. Being mannequin thin is primarily a First-World ideal. I cannot think of anything related to body standards that has been unchanging.

FM: What forces these changes in your opinion? From "The Birth of Venus" (c. 1486) by Botticelli to Marie Antoinette, Louise Brooks, Bettie Page, Twiggy, Kim Kardashian...

HK: For a meaningful answer to this, I think you need to go to an evolutionary biologist. From my non-scholarly perspective, it is simply another manifestation of humanity's quest for change.

Idiosyncrasy and distinction make for a visual allure. Whenever a publication does the photo conflation of the faces of stars of the period in an attempt to find a generic ideal, the result is inevitably undistinguished. The subtle deviations that contribute to a charismatic specialness are folded into a bland physiognomy of shared commonality.

FM: We have been desperately exploring or trying to re-define the silhouette for centuries now. Humans have been working on reconstructing the body and proportion through clothing... Why this particular need?

HK: Western fashion since the fourteenth century has marshalled the human impulse to novelty with the notion of privilege and class. Innovation is associated with individuals of affluence and power with the ability to take on transformations unconstrained by cost, whether as originators or early adapters. There have been certain counter-currents, such as the Italian notion of "sprezzatura", Beau Brummell's fastidious minimalism, or Chanel's inverting of class-generated aesthetic codes, but overall, fashion succeeds because of the status association of being early, if not first, on trends.

EMOTION

FM: How can we manoeuvre emotion through fashion?

HK: The main emotion most designers aspiring to commercial viability try to elicit is joy. There are exceptions. When Rei Kawakubo and Yohji Yamamoto presented their all black collections in Paris in the early eighties, many critics found the défilés sad and apocalyptic.

In all candor, the only fashion that I find intrinsically emotional is the work of Alexander McQueen. It communicates the sense of extreme beauty forged on a crucible of immense psychic pain. I think even without knowing anything about the designer, one sees the transcendent psychological richness of his designs.

On a more mundane level, I suppose the uniforms of bridal apparel, and until recently, mourning apparel convey through the severely constrained codes of their forms, the possibility of importing emotion through the fact of their context and function.

All of this of course is from the perspective of an observer, someone looking at fashion. Someone wearing fashion might derive all kinds of emotions from a given garment.

FM: Why is the ceremonial process of dressing linked with achieving a higher state of feelings?

HK: There is the scene at the end of the Glenn Close version of "Dangerous Liaisons" where, socially shunned, she removes her make-up. The façade has been broken and she is destroyed.

Dressing is the reverse. We put on our clothes, often quickly and mindlessly, but on occasion with specific intent. What we wear, what we choose to wear, defines our role as a social creature. When there is no disjunction between who we want to represent ourselves to be, and how we appear, there is confidence. Dressing is speech, articulating who we are, or at least who we want everyone else to believe we are.

FM: Where in your opinion fashion meets with emotion?

HK: Fashion meets emotion in our direct relationship with clothes. It is an element in the construction of our individual personas.

Since clothes are intimately tied to who we are, there is often an emotional association with their connection to events in our lives. Looking through the closets of anyone is as revelatory as reading their diary. An emotional component can be evoked in the signature style of the wearer, since the articles of dress are intimate and explicit evidence of the life of the wearer. I would go as far as to say clothes can function as a surrogate for the absent individual. I think of Joseph Beuys' felt suit, or Corbusier's eyeglasses. The emotional components of fashion are mostly allusive or associative rather than intrinsic.

FM: In your experience as an academic, putting together so many wonderful exhibitions, catalogues and outstanding projects... I wonder if you were interested in observing people visiting your "stories" and at which point they would feel most vulnerable?

HK: As a curator, I always functioned rather selfishly and chose to address topics and concepts that interested me personally at the time. Still, the ultimate goal always was to educate the viewer, the public, by engaging them with subjects they might not have thought to investigate on their own.

There is a difference between the galleries of costume exhibitions and the galleries focused on the other fine and applied arts. No matter how popular a traditional artist, their galleries are generally quiet, the public approaching the work with a kind of pre-ordained reverence, even if they do not like the work. With apparel, even historic examples, everyone who wears clothing comes in with a very pronounced sense of authority and personal knowledge. Subjective responses are articulated loudly because there is no sense of deference to clothing designs, even work that they might not fully comprehend.

Instead, one hears, "I'd NEVER wear that", or "Oh, my God! I would kill for that dress." In that sense, the costume audience is not in a position of vulnerability. They assess fashion with the confidence of active participants in the medium.

FM: How can we overcome ourselves through dressing while avoiding obsolescence?

HK: People who say there are immutable characteristics of good or bad taste do not acknowledge the constantly evolving nature of aesthetics. An individual can have a primary and signature style that they feel is best for them, but even the most reductive elements of dress can subtly incorporate the more ephemeral trends. To avoid obsolescence is to fight the impulse to stasis, and mediate the uncompromising aspects of one's taste with modifications reflecting the contemporary Zeitgeist. The alternative is to choose to be so eccentric and idiosyncratic (essentially wearing a costume) that the effect is outside of fashion completely.

FM: What determines if something is surprising or emotional enough on the catwalk?

HK: Rather than pursuing a laugh, the designer would like to precipitate desire. Mrs. Vreeland described a Balenciaga presentation where the designer proposed a nude body stocking. She said one client was so astonished and moved that, and I'll have to paraphrase, "She slid off her chair to the ground in froth and foam." McQueen did that.

FM: Why some fashion shows are better than others?

HK: The best are a totality of concept with every element in the production enhancing and supporting the clothes. But most important are the clothes themselves. The dramatics of John Galliano's Dior shows, and McQueen's, were breathtaking in their construction of an alternate reality. Thom Browne's presentations have an uncanny quality.

But I also remember my first Ronaldus Shamask défilé. It was late in starting. The editors smoked then, so the room was a thick cigarette haze. A pianist was playing: finally, he stopped. Lights went out, the runway lights came up and Sayoko emerged with a T-shaped coat. The room was absolutely silent except for the photographers who rose in an undulating wave as she walked down the catwalk. The flash of their cameras and the clicks of the lenses filled the space. The simplicity and purity of the moment, this was repeated for the whole show, of the rising and subsiding bodies of the photographers lining the runway and only the sound of their clicking cameras and flashes going off documenting the pure architectural simplicity of the clothes. It was enough.

FM: How does expression serve fashion?

HK: The best designers are seducers. They create desire for things that, from a certain point of view, are not essential to our survival. And yet, fashion, as an ephemeral project, can be like a tweet, a very quick notation of society and culture, politics and economics, at a precise moment. Other manifestations of applied and fine arts take more time. What fashion lacks in durability it makes up in the immediacy of its relevance.

From a personal perspective, fashion is the language we speak when we leave the privacy of our homes. It is, as I've said earlier, communication. Even if we consider you don't think about what you wear, you are projecting that sentiment. It is still a position vis-à-vis fashion that you are presenting. What we wear is broadcasting who we are. The great communicators in this medium align intention with expression.

My attitude has always been a variation of Chanel's dictum. Always dress as if you will run into your next lover, or your greatest enemy, even if it is to walk your dog in the morning. In fact, especially if it is to walk your dog in the morning.

POLITICS

FM: How is fashion revelatory of the social mechanism and politics?

HK: Economic hierarchies, caste, gender, ethnicity, cultural affinities, etc., can all be conveyed through what we wear. It is interesting to look at renderings of utopian apparel. Often it is meant to be based on democratic principles so the relatively un-gendered styles of classical dress are alluded to, or the tabard-style robes of the medieval era, as if a somewhat untailored silhouette is de-sexed and less hierarchical. In the opposite, dystopian dress, the references might also have an element of uniformity, but there it functions as a means of repressing the individual into anonymity, merged into a vast collective. The uniform is interesting in that it submits an individual to an immediately identifiable group. The group identity overrides the individual identity.

In the military, it functions to establish hierarchy and status. The paradox is that by dressing everyone alike, but accruing small elements of distinction to individuals of higher authority, the military uniform asserts status while simultaneously obliterating the individual. (The exception, and there are always exceptions, is at the highest levels of authority individuals can, like General Patton, customise the template of their outfits.)

In the early eighties, I was at Charles de Gaulle where a group of Chinese bureaucrats were standing together, men and women. The "Mao" suits they wore were ostensibly identical and genderless as the women wore pants. But each one had on a different colour — dark blue, black, grey, dark brown, dark green — of gabardine. If you really examined them, they all had rolled collars, but some had points and others had rounded their collar tips. Like school kids in Japan who wear uniforms, but individualise them by proportion and silhouette (a shorter sleeve, a higher hemmed cuff, a baggier cut), the Chinese officials had very subtly personalised their uniforms. They conformed to the rules, but modified the details.

FM: What about the way fashion is formed today? Who is directing it?

HK: The Western high fashion system is undergoing a shift, a total tectonic shift. Fashion can still be trickled down, but increasingly it percolates upward. The Web has transformed the dissemination of fashion and individual style. The traditional sources and gatekeepers of fashion — the designers, the editors, the buyers, and merchants — no longer have an exclusive pipeline to fashion. Also, the proliferation of global design brands has created a wildly heterogeneous mix of appropriate fashions. The very plenitude of options has diffused the power of the traditional system to direct fashion. It certainly no longer dictates. In this new and evolving environment, "style influencers" and smaller storefront design houses can sometimes gain a foothold outside the huge commercial fashion business.

Meanwhile, brick and mortar stores and glossy monthlies are confronting changing patterns of how people select and shop for apparel. The fashion system isn't exactly breaking apart, but it is splitting into an interconnected network of febrile elements. It is an exciting time when everyone is looking for a viable new paradigm.

FM: The ways models present fashions on the catwalk change every decade. It seems that in the past we had ceremonial moments, at times very lively, dance was even incorporated on the runway, etc.

HK: Fashion runway presentations are like music. Trends come and go.

FM: We witness how a model's posture has changed, the use of hands, and the choreography that is now a rather straight walking line. How would you explain this phenomenon?

HK: Some of it historically was related to what was being worn. A film clip of models in the pre-World War I Poiret period is surprising for the cloddishness of their movements. In the fifties, the house models of the "cabine" would present the collection in the salons of a couture house with numbered cards in their gloved hands. In the sixties, young designers without couture affiliations held shows similar to the art happenings of the period. Rock music and models that responded to the soundtrack animated the clothes. The Battle of Versailles presentation (1973) is evidence of a dramatic shift in modes of presentation. The French did tableaux vivants with mannequins as backdrops for their many stars, but the Americans used the relaxed and self- choreographed moves of their models, many African-American, as a participatory chorus to their one star, Liza Minnelli. It was the hauteur of the French mannequins versus the natural swagger of the Americans. But things date. Pat Cleveland's famous pirouettes that animated the runways of the seventies and early eighties seemed as camp as disco by the early nineties.

FM: Not more than twenty years ago, designers such as McQueen and John Galliano were creating entire collections inspired by tribes, global historical references and folklore. Today this approach is considered inappropriate. What happened in between?

HK: I'm not the one to ask about this. I honestly feel like I am too calcified by the past to be on the right side of the present. I do think that certain manifestations of cultural appropriation are wrongheaded, but I wish our response to it could be more nuanced. For example, in contemporary art criticism Gauguin has become increasingly controversial and problematical. The idea of power relationships and the racist colonial lens has informed considerations of various historical and contemporary cultural citations, but I also see, despite the implicit period sexism and racism, that beauty and new ideas can come from an intersection of cultures. Would we prefer that Gauguin's renderings of his personalised view of Tahiti did not exist, however fraught by the shadow of a kind of sex tourism (my anachronistic interpretation) and colonial privilege? Since every culture has self-identifying markers, should each culture also have complete and exclusive possession and control of the use and interpretation of its ideas, artefacts, and history? There will always be the possibility of inappropriate citation and application, even of crude exploitation, but I am an outlier in believing that quotation and allusion by individuals outside a culture enrich more than diminish our global cultural vocabulary, and thus are worth the risks of the downside.

FM: Today, we experience the phenomenon of the "designer tribe": Balmain, Rick Owens, Yohji Yamamoto, Comme des Garçons, Ann Demeulemeester, Dries Van Noten...?
How does this uniformity affect the society and how different designer uniformity is from working or school uniforms?

HK: This question brings us back less to the notion of tribes than the idea of the fragmentation of fashion. To me, this moment is exciting and healthy (others might characterise it as chaotic and feverish), as we are in a world where so many distinct and original voices can have commercial viability.

I am sure there are a small number of people who are loyal to one defined aesthetic and one and only one designer or house, but it seems much more common to find people who construct their own look by cherry-picking the offerings of a cluster of designers who might share certain techniques or sensibilities. Those individuals might look like they are part of the Miuccia or Rei, or Dries tribe, but they are in fact lone wolves.

I cannot think of another time in the last 300 years when one could be considered fashionably attired in so many dramatically different and contrasting ways.

FM: In your opinion does the longevity of these "tribes" depend on the creative timeline of the designer's relevancy or will it be infinite?

HK: Interesting to consider. It is my experience that most designers have a fecund period of up to three decades, maybe slightly more, often much less. It is only a hypothesis, but I think since fashion is necessarily rooted in the world, that as designers get older, their formidable accrual of experiences does make up for their estrangement from and connectedness to contemporary life. In their twenties-thirties they are living the life they are designing for. After, not so much. They can still be important designers, but I think their relevance begins to fade and is relinquished to emerging talents. Also, so much fashion is about the desire to be desired. Like everything the elements of allure change over time. Designers can have younger staff around them contributing their thoughts, but ultimately they are channelling that part of life second hand through the filter of others.

There is nothing like being in the world of the unattached looking to be attached to understand one of the root impulses of fashion: to be found attractive and be desired.

FM: At what level are we conscious of what we see, buy or wear? Does it matter?

HK: Some people are more conscious than others. There is no great icon of style who is not consciously (or eventually intuitively) making decisions about dress. As I've said before, fashion is a language. What we wear is a text. We should all have in the back of our minds as we dress that we are expressing something of ourselves without words. As an act of communication, it is often the first impression, before we speak. It seems to me it is important to aspire to be clear in all our efforts at communication.

If we are compelled to dissemble and deceive, it is even more imperative that we are conscious of our decisions regarding dress. Noel Coward said to Cecil Beaton regarding the latter's apparent effeminacy, "A polo jumper or unfortunate tie exposes one to danger."

MICHÈLE LAMY

Partner Rick Owens

BODY

FILEP MOTWARY: You earlier told me that "fashion is a great reflection of its time — is and has been for a while — a precursor / forerunner of our emotional state. And the runways are here to prove it." You mention the lack of top models, the merge of boys and girls models within shows as well as the experimentation or the acceptance of a third gender that is now forming the Zeitgeist. How did we come to this level, not only in fashion but also in general?

MICHÈLE LAMY: The world went through many evolutions in the past, I think that right now we notice these changes even more because of Trump. His actions enabled women, minorities to react, to show their strength, the gay people to react because his politics are a threat to our rights as humans.

Of course these issues are not new, but having someone like Trump as the president of the country of all countries raised even more reactions from people who want to secure things the previous generations fought so hard for! You see this reaction on the streets, in fashion, the social media and everywhere; there is an evolution in society that is important and normally fashion is the first to show it. Information is shared so rapidly now through applications like Instagram and everything is open to many more people than ever before. What is happening now with the supremacists is no accident, as it appeared to be at first. It's perhaps like boxing, metaphorically speaking. If everybody wants to fight there will always be fights. In boxing, when you want to fight it is at least one on one and there are a lot of rules that will decree you a winner or a loser.

I just finished a project, a performance/installation based on boxing that was presented at Selfridges under the name "What are we fighting for?" Boxing can serve as a metaphor for so many things like art or music for example, because it connects you with others, you can look each other in the eye and be connected on the same level, and say "we must stay strong and stand for what we believe in." Even though I have been boxing for forty years without absolutely no chance to fight or even to think about it, I understand it's like playing chess. You look at your opponent in the eye and predict his/her move.

The question I am trying to raise and get the answer — "What are we fighting for?" — is also a statement. At this time it is a phenomenon to watch the champions and what they wear to fight in the ring. This is a question that I am asking myself too, specifically in my curatorial role for my Lamyland X Selfridges project, that was indeed about the body, it was political and about emotion too! It was on from January/February and into March 2018.

FM: How is the meaning of the "body" approached in contemporary fashion, considering its permanent outline and the fact that it is something generic? Are designers today connected to the body they design for?

ML: I will start with Rick. When you wear his clothes you already start walking in a different way, there are so many aspects of his work that emphasise on certain attributes of the body, the tight arms, etc. He focuses on the body but he does not follow a classic way to communicate with it.

The body is his starting point, he starts from there but what he is truly interested in is the way it moves. At the same time I think that all designers follow the body, each in his/her own way. Look at Rei [Kawakubo]! Even if her work is more sculptures rather than clothes, she presents the body in her own personal way. The body allows us to approach its proportions, work on them and reshape it, shorten or elongate it. In a way the dressed body becomes the personal message you want to communicate to the outside. If you want to show the body as much as you can, do it through clothes.

FM: What does clothing serve today? How connected is society to the clothes we choose to wear? Does it matter to be conscious with what we wear?

ML: I'm going to give you an example, Edith Blayney, whom I would meet at the gym and we later became friends. It was during the first year we moved to Paris with Rick. She came to the show and at the time she would always dress in men's collections, as it was her style, Dior Homme and all the rest. One day she changed everything and became a fan of Rick Owens and she wears him in her very own way.

Things happen sometimes to some of us, we finally come across what is destined to come our way and without a question we welcome it in our lives. Her body did not change, she has an incredible allure but through Rick she found a way to connect with her emotions and be even closer to her inner self.

FM: What about the way you dress, the way you paint your fingers, your golden teeth caps... what does each of these incredible attributes say about you and did you decide to enrich or underline your look?

ML: Hmm, this is the real story. I got absolutely seduced by the Berbers, who are an ethnic group indigenous to North Africa, during my first trip there. I was so mesmerised by the tattoos they had on their faces, being very young at the time, 17 or 18 I was. Also, I have this constitutional look, being very tanned so it kind of looks natural on me. When I was a little girl, with my sister and my dad at the Riviera, people would speak to us in English as they thought we were Indians because of our dark skin and our very long hair while our father looked almost like a Gandhi type, with no hair.

The way I looked even as a child created some sort of personal evolution and I would experiment early as well, like with henna to change the colour of my hair, or to tattoo my fingers so that I could look at them. Then I moved to the dye because I wanted my nails to be black but not in a cheap shiny way.

The teeth happened in L.A., where I found this artist that was a new-age type who convinced me to put gold on them. My God, I spent all this money, you cannot even see anything [laughs]. So I thought "Why didn't I just do one in the front and then the rest?" This is my personal evolution though. You know, I could not have long nails for example, because I would not be able to take off my contact lenses all the time. Rick says: "Fashion is a quiet opportunity to participate and communicate. First impressions can be significant, and I like the idea of putting your best foot forward. The effort to charm is generous and never hurts." And I say: "What are we fighting for?"

If boxing could be perceived as barbaric (as my black fingers and tattoos on the face), it is in fact a metaphor for looking at the bigger picture of where we are at in the world and how we can stand up and face what we need to change. Through the use of fashion and art around this subject, I aim to open up a broader dialogue of how we can use our bodies to connect with our emotions and influence our politics for the better.

FM: On the occasion of the Rick Owens exhibition, how would you say exhibiting fashion serves in understanding the body? What about our society?

ML: It is interesting to see fashion presented outside the fashion show context and to be exhibited in a museum as something more static. But to me fashion shows are very important for the designer, for his followers, for the emotions reflected within. This exhibition of Rick is very much about the designer, it's very much about his talent and his craft. He has shown at the Milan Triennale from 15 December 2017 to 25 March 2018 — a true insight into where he is at in the world of fashion.

The exhibition was more about fashion as a mirror of our times, his style, the clothing he makes. I am not sure how people who are not in fashion saw it but I hope they were surprised. The body serves fashion shows, the streets, and daily life.

EMOTION

FM: What is so important about being new? Does creation have to be new?

ML: Creation is about new, otherwise it's something else.

FM: How can we manoeuvre emotion through fashion?

ML: Rick is a great example of incorporating emotion in his work, in a fashion show. The thing that changed in fashion is that individual models are disappearing into being one thing. Even if you separate and look at them individually, the meaning today is more about groups or tribes, even small ones, instead of individualism. Presenting as it used to be has changed a lot. Models are no longer carrying the clothes, smiling and dancing.

At Rick's shows you want to cry, most of the times you do not know the reasons but the emotions are so strong that they hit on a very unpredictable moment and you let your feelings out free. It's not a cry for the beauty you see but more about the emotion you get.

To quote Rick again: "I always like it when the barbaric turns elegant and controlled."

And Joyce Carol Oates wrote of the Noble Art, in her "On Boxing":

"[Boxing is primitive] as birth, death, and erotic love might be said to be primitive, and forces on reluctant acknowledgment that the most profound experiences of our lives are physical events — though we believe ourselves to be, and surely are, essentially spiritual beings."

FM: And at which point fashion makes us feel vulnerable?

ML: This is a very personal state for each of us and very independent. If you are not true to yourself, this is when vulnerability comes to play.

FM: Why is it important to have the feeling of belonging?

ML: When we are walking as a tribe, we advance, we push further the limits and barriers of any kind, we evolve, we change into a better version of ourselves, together and much stronger. The whole world is a tribe, as I see it. In every tribe you have different people but then, they all have things that are common. This is not fashion I am referring to though. It's the emotions and the politics that can form a tribe and clothes are the tools we use to show where we belong.

POLITICS

FM: How can personal become global? You mentioned that using art and fashion we can open broader dialogues for the use of our bodies to connect with our emotions and influence our politics.

ML: To be in your body you need to be conscious. There's got to be a connection between the two. If you have that then you have a way of processing your emotions in a healthier and constructive way. Achieving that ability would automatically inform your politics, individually. If everybody seeks for that connection with our inner self-politics, things will be more moral, more constructive.

FM: How does fashion serve liberty and vice versa?

ML: In a lot of Arabic countries, fashion is antifashion as women are forced to wear certain things in certain ways. In the Emirates, people are so proud to wear their traditional costume. When you are there you see them hiding behind these clothes but not necessarily for the reasons we think. This sort of traditional fashion these people follow reflects the politics directly in our face!

I thought it was so stupid of France for example when they put this law about the Islamic veil while at the same time you have the Catholic nuns walking around with those enormous headpieces. It didn't make much sense to me.

So, it's a fact that politics are getting through us by using fashion now, as it was always done of course, yet now it's more official.

At this point I think Kim Kardashian is another great example of the contemporary culture. The other day in London, a friend of mine who is a soccer player took me out to a club. I was shocked to see that every single girl in the club was a Kim Kardashian lookalike and it was very difficult for me to decide if their bottoms were results of plastic surgery or if they wore some kind of padding to achieve that look. It was amazing. Imagine thirty-five Kims in the same place. Overall it's an extraordinary phenomenon and very interesting. Kim Kardashian is very pragmatic, as I know a bit of her in person, and she is someone that changed our culture in the recent years.

Some artists did it in the past, like Orlan for example, but that was on a different scale compared to the impact Kim has on the contemporary society.

FM: How are myths in fashion getting developed around certain subjects or people? How does fantasy serve reality? Should it,

in contemporary culture? Is there room for nuance, fantasy and extravagance?

ML: It could be irrelevant now and perhaps tomorrow someone does an extravagant show as such and is automatically considered as the best! This is something that can change at any given moment. We still have some of this extravagance today, for example Karl Lagerfeld's version of Chanel but I am not sure it's the same — it is still extravagance, only in a different way.

When John Travolta was doing his dance routines back in the day, his vest became so popular on a global level.

There will always be things that touch you more than others and there will always be myths; it's their meaning that changes depending on the context we experience them through.

Kim Kardashian's reality is others people's fantasy and especially now with the social media; we build our own myths that can fit into the square photo Instagram allows you to upload.

FM: You have worked within a ready-to-wear designer approach, as much as with designing furniture alongside Rick Owens. How do these different approaches go together? How do you see the body in relation to the furniture?

ML: We started this project from home and our personal needs to dress the environment we lived in, to be able to behave as ourselves. Even if this is a collection that is sold in galleries, it comes from our home and the way me and Rick like to sit, to work, to read or relax but everything in relation to our bodies. It's also very personal.

THIERRY-MAXIME LORIOT

Curator, author, storyteller

BODY

FILEP MOTWARY: According to Dr. Anthony Synnott's book "The Body Social" originally published in 1993, the transformations the body goes through in time also affect one's self and change it. How is the meaning of the "body" approached in fashion today, considering its permanent outline and the fact that it is something generic?

THIERRY-MAXIME LORIOT: I am glad you quote a Montreal professor from Concordia University! Synnott works on the idea that the body is a "social creation", which I think is true as it is an evolution of something given by birth that you can decide to change, modify and that you in fact are the only to master its evolution. I am not a specialist of social psychology and identities, but in fashion studies the approach of the body — even if as you say is generic — is clearly that fashion can also play a role: as the element that can connect human beings together and with society.

In his essay "Taste and Fashion: The Social Function of Fashion and Style", Finnish sociologist Jukka Gronow wrote on the idea of individuality:

"[...] fashion is a societal formation always combining two opposite forces. It is a socially acceptable and safe way to distinguish oneself from others and, at the same time, it satisfies the individual's need for social adaptation and imitation. Fashion helps to solve — at least provisionally — the central problem of the philosophy of life, also expressed in the antinomy of taste as formulated by Kant. It teaches the modern man how a person can be a homogeneous part of a social mass without losing his individuality, or how he can both stick to his own private taste and expect others — who recognizably also have a taste of their own — to share it. Fashion helps to overcome the distance between an individual and his society [...]."

All these theories are valid, as it can be seen from different point of views in time, and will have an evolution that not only has to do with fashion but mostly with culture and backgrounds and how they create a distance or a proximity with fashion. We are all humans who need to feel. In her essay "Addressing the Body", Joanne Entwistle wrote that "Dress is a basic fact of social life and this, according to anthropologists, is true of all known human cultures: all people 'dress' the body in some way, be it through clothing, tattooing, cosmetics or other forms of body painting. To put it another way, no culture leaves the body unadorned but adds to, embellishes, enhances or decorates the body. [...] Dress is the way in which individuals learn to live in their bodies and feel at home in them."

FM: More than ever before, fashion and the society in general are now dealing with new type of bodies while gender is also frontline. Why in your opinion? (these subjects are not new).

TML: It is quite simply related to the evolution of society. Religion played a big role in portraying what was to be considered wrong or right and was acceptable — good, bad, evil — according to the Bible. In North America as well as in Europe, churches are now empty and mentalities changed and what was considered a mental disorder, from homosexuality to being transgender is now thankfully accepted and pretty common. There is still a lot of work to do but the guilt related to it is gone and the new generations have witnessed these changes and have a more open vision of society. Some designers, like Jean Paul Gaultier, used their fashion as a social message, a mirror of society to tell the truth with their clothes. He was a true pioneer in showing objectified men, transgenders, effeminate guys, gay couples on his catwalk. Same with legend Madonna via her music, videos and concerts. She is one of the first if not the first woman to speak freely about sexuality, freedom, homosexuality, desire, AIDS, gender and many other social issues, and greatly contributed in helping change perception of things by being this powerful woman who did not need a man. All these elements contributed to the acceptance of new genders.

FM: What would be your prediction of the future body? The technological body, the body that is dressed by computerised clothing. Why does the body still need to look and act human?

TML: When I was a kid, I thought that by year 2000 we would all live in space but this never happened! I do not think that the technological body will ever happen. I think fabrics for example will just get better and better with time, more efficient. Now the materials used in the winter are thinner and as warm as a down jacket, you have fabrics that repel completely liquids, fireproof technology on fabrics changed.

FM: How connected are fashion designers today to the body they design for?

TML: I think real couture belongs to a past generation of couturiers who would really use the body to create their clothes. Jean Paul Gaultier, for example, works directly with the body, with the real fabrics, to make his collections at his studio, the opposite of most of the other designers who always use toiles.

Others like Viktor & Rolf for example, do not design with a certain woman in mind — their work is more about creation and closer to art as Deyan Sudjic mentioned in his book "The Language of Things", that the less useful a garment is the closest to art it is. I am not saying that Viktor & Rolf clothes are useless — rather the opposite — but that they are very much an outlier of couture and fashion as they do not design with any commercial concerns or intentions.

They will never do the classic collection with pretty daywear and nice gowns that hopefully will end up on a red carpet or push for accessories. It is solely about the idea and the conceptualisation of clothes. A designer like Iris van Herpen is inventing new forms and uses new technologies to create works of art with radical materials often printed in three dimensions.

FM: You are behind three major fashion curatorial projects, the monographic exhibitions of Viktor & Rolf, the uber successful Jean Paul Gaultier exhibition and your newest one of Thierry Mugler to be open soon in Canada. All these design houses are known for their incredible ways to dress body, in a totally personal manner that later became universal. Would you kindly share with us how each of them approaches the body, their differences and perhaps similarities?

TML: I would say in fact that the most similar in terms of approach to the body, to humans are definitely Jean Paul Gaultier and the German photographer Peter Lindbergh, with whom I also did an exhibition titled "A Different Vision on Fashion Photography". They both broke taboos in the fashion industry by using non-conventional models and being very different, completely opposite to what was trendy in their times. Gaultier cherishes different body shapes and origins. He will create a dress according to the model's skin colour, to her freckles, to her hair colour, the body is definitely one of his main inspiration, and I think this explains why everybody loved him so much. It is because he showed reality and many recognised themselves in his work for its accessibility. Gaultier often worked on creating garments that mimicked the human silhouette, with incredible bodysuits that were embroidered with pearls to recreate veins and also costumes he did for Pedro Almodovar's movie "The Skin I Live" In which were all inspired by the body.

The work of Thierry Mugler is as distinctive as it is avant-garde. It has an architectural, hyper-feminised style that sublimates the curves of the femme fatale and imposing men with broad shoulders. This designer knows how to distinguish himself through constant innovation and audacious silhouettes that have marked an era and found a place in the history of fashion like Gaultier and Viktor & Rolf. You immediately recognise their work without even looking at the labels. Mugler's singular style, a futurist version of "New Look" with a touch of fantasy and fetishism, is still a powerful influence on today's generation of couturiers. His ironic stance on eroticism had many fashion insiders misunderstanding some of his collections, and he remains a controversial figure in the fashion industry on how he was modifying the body by exaggerating the shoulders, clinching the waist, etc. Mugler's creative impulse has always been to transform, even transhumanising, the body, and his spectacular creations have often been considered extreme, unwearable and too constrictive. He would invent animals, creatures and robots, by devising chrome bustiers and plexiglass bodysuits, padded shoulders and radically enhanced body shapes.

It was a world of fantasy, something that Viktor & Rolf do not do, as they propose a fashion that is less body centred and more conceptual. Their ideas do not work around muses (it did once with Tilda Swinton and her clones) and does not reflect a rejection of the body but states an approach that is more intellectual. Viktor & Rolf are the only couturiers I know who start creating a collection when they have found the idea for the show. The presentation will in fact launch the idea behind the collection, which is certainly unique and very daring. It somehow reveals that neither the human body nor the fashion industry inspire them. For sure, one thing Gaultier, Mugler and Viktor & Rolf have in common is that they do not follow trends, they initiate them and have already left a considerable influence in fashion history.

FM: Being a fashion curator, what would be your observation, your verdict on the body? How does the body behave within the walls of the museum context and how on the outside, as part of the society?

TML: Inside the museum, depending on the subject exhibited, the body can play a crucial role. In the Jean Paul Gaultier exhibition we worked with Denis Marleau and Stéphanie Jasmin from the theatre company

UBU in Montreal to create these animated mannequins. Some questioned their use, but in this case, the world of Gaultier is based on diversity, different bodies, different origins and it was very important to include it to understand how his fashion was open and generous. So all shapes and skin tones were represented with the mannequins on which projection were made on moulds of the heads of actual muses of the designer and even of Gaultier himself who was telling his own story. One of the mannequin was quoting Roland Barthes with his 1967 book "The Fashion System". The following is a quote from this book summing it all up: "[...] Clothing concerns all of the human person, all of the body, all of the relationships of man to body as well as the relationships of the body to society [...]."

FM: How connected is society to the clothes they choose to wear? Do we seek for a deeper meaning into clothing?

TML: Everybody wants or try one day to stand out and be individualised with what they wear. This phenomenon always existed from dandies, hippies, power dressing, to punks, that one can identify with a group in society with his clothes but also express a political point of view and a social status. When you are younger your style is more related to your cultural background, which tends to disappear with time, and ultimately with age you dress more for yourself.

EMOTION

FM: Can a piece of garment embody emotional tension?

TML: I think in her book "Sex and Suits", Ann Hollander describes it quite nicely when she writes that "Insisting further on the theme of sex, men and women began to dress extremely differently from each other somewhere during the fourteenth century, having worked up to it rather slowly during the two before. After that, the borrowing of visual motifs across a visual sharper sexual divide created more suggestive interest and emotional tension in clothing than it ever could have done when men and women wore similarly designed garments. Small suggestions of transvestism became more noticeable and more exciting."

I think sexuality and difference between man and woman are the key elements of that emotional tension you can find in fashion. Jean Paul Gaultier played with these themes a lot in the eighties often reversing the gender roles of men and women and by giving the power to women with certain elements, for example the inside pocket in a jacket that you would only find in men's clothes as traditionally they were the ones paying — Gaultier always put an inside pocket in his women's jacket to say that women can also pay for men. Same with his skirts for me. Historically, just like the corsets worn by dandies for their posture, men in skirt is something that was taboo only in Occidental fashion, as if you have a minimum of general culture you know that men have been wearing different variations of skirts through history and still now, in many different cultures, from sarongs and pareos to kilts and the Sumerian men's skirts.

FM: At which point fashion makes us feel vulnerable?

TML: Fashion can make us feel vulnerable when it shows, reveals something personal, too much of the body or a weakness. The vulnerability often comes from the behaviour of other people, how they react to certain stimuli, it can also be a cultural reaction to garments whether it is linked to religious beliefs or traditions. Many situations can emerge linked to clothes and bring this vulnerability from being different depending on your gender, your skin colour, your religion — it is also about acceptance in society, having an open vision. Other elements can bring vulnerability when people are wearing tight-fitting clothes, are displaying a sexual fetish — for example wearing SM attire or else — or reveal human shapes that are sexually connoted and can bring discomfort to the others. I wish everyone had the freedom to dress as they want, we are slowly getting there in big cities.

FM: I wonder if you were interested in observing people visiting your "stories" and at which point they would feel most vulnerable? How can you manoeuvre emotion through your work?

TML: I often visit exhibitions I curated just to see what people say and comment, it is always very interesting to hear people's comments about your vision of another artist. I love to work with living artists, all my experiences have been very positive so far, from Jean Paul Gaultier with whom I did fifteen exhibitions so far, to Viktor & Rolf and Thierry Mugler that are very open and incredibly generous. I think these fashion artists are not insecure about their work and also the fact that they have nothing to prove and can consent on having a point of view that complements their work rather than differentiate it, is important. The fashion of these three is very different but they have tons of similarities in terms of the social aspect, even their approach to Haute Couture is very democratic. Viktor & Rolf love exhibitions as they are the only way the public can see their work. Seeing the public as they are moved, shocked or any other reaction is something I enjoy watching, just like when you watch a movie and the actor moves you, the director did something right. It is not about my work, I consider myself a storyteller; the designers are the main actors and their stories, their acts are the galleries.

FM: There are certain ways of presenting fashion, I will focus on the fashion show and the art of exhibiting fashion: what are the differences and similarities as you see it and where does emotion fit in?

TML: I think it is important to find the message you want to convey and make it very clear whether it is a fashion show or an exhibition. The fashion show has a commercial aspect 99 per cent of the time, the exhibition should tell a story. It is not always the case in both, as some designers do only Haute Couture and do not sell any of their clothes, sometimes only to collectors and museums, sometimes nothing. The exhibition and museification of designers and fashion is now a cultural phenomenon that has changed a lot in the past ten years as many brands saw an opportunity to sell more perfumes and accessories by gaining the prestige and visibility of a museum exhibition. The brand-sponsored exhibition often brings a vision that is solely based on the iconification of the brand and has a commercial meaning; many museums now host this type of exhibition as they allow them to produce other exhibitions that otherwise would lack financing. Fashion shows can bring emotions just like exhibitions but on a different level. If you take for example Alexander McQueen who through his fashion shows brought many emotions by the way he staged them and stimulated the public with his approach to certain topics, I would say his exhibitions presented at the Met and at the V&A are a perfect example of how you can experience the same or similar emotions with what people experienced while attending his fashion shows back in the day. This is one of the most beautiful fashion exhibitions I have ever seen. Some people have been touched by Gaultier, others have not — I think it is a very personal approach which is also closely linked to memories and connections that can be made with our senses.

FM: How does fashion comment about the way we live?

TML: Fashion can often be interpreted as a statement and as a social status "guide". From belonging to specific groups, from ghetto kids, to rich housewives, to businessmen, to students, with age we all go through phases of self-identification through fashion and go for utterly importance to non-existent.

FM: Could we suggest clothing is a living organism? If yes, in what ways?

TML: I think we should take more of a scientific approach here as I do not think it is something anyone is ready to do. I would not. Clothes, from cotton to leather, are transformed living organisms already...

POLITICS

FM: Why do we exhibit fashion in museums, apart from the financial and historical reasons?

TML: Times are changing and fashion is part of the movements of society, so it is a new media just like video art, that was not shown in museums last century but now is included in permanent collections and exhibitions programming. I do not do exhibitions for financial reasons. The museums I work with — for example The Montreal Museum of Fine Arts with its director Nathalie Bondil — initiate and produce exhibitions on artists, not on brands. Bondil is behind the Jean Paul Gaultier historical world tour (2011–16), the Thierry Mugler exhibitions I both curated (2019) and the Yves Saint Laurent exhibition (2009). None of these exhibitions were financed by the brand. Not one cent. Same with Viktor & Rolf at the National Gallery of Victoria in Melbourne — it was completely financed by sponsors and donors. There is a difference; for the past two decades, starting with Giorgio Armani at the Guggenheim in 2001, it was controversial because of the way it was financed — Armani self-financed his event. Now we see a lot of brands who want to promote themselves and elevate their prestige with museum exhibitions.

Even nowadays when you see famous French luxury brands, not to name them, that have all these touring exhibitions in emerging markets, showcasing perfume ads as big as the building and having an exhibition gift shop as big as the exhibition to sell bags and accessories, you understand that these ones are not based on the richness of the content but it is more a placement and a strategy of empowerment and bringing the brand to an iconic level. When you think about it financially, to create an exhibition or to buy pages of advertising in a magazine or billboards in the street, it can cost almost the same. The exhibition stays part of the story of the house, the magazine goes in the recycling bin. Olivier Gabet, the Director of Musée des Arts Décoratifs in Paris, was very open and honest about the financing of the brands. For him, it was a question of survival of his institution and of making possible the birth of other less "popular" per se projects. His Dior exhibition presented in 2017 was a great example, a spectacular scenography, a rich content and a great success with 700,000 visitors: this exhibition, made possible with the help of Dior, proves that you can do both, have a rich academic and historical content and make money.

Most museums are non-profit institutions and have to self-finance with their development teams looking for sponsors and patrons who make these projects possible or rely on the government. The way exhibitions are built and presented now, in a society filled with social media and clicks for "likes" or "don't like", museum have the pressure to present a "product" that stands out and attracts crowds. Big crowds. In the past years, movie theatres, bookstores, music stores closed down, everything is online, at home and individualised. It needs extra efforts to be able to bring visitors to the doors of your institution when you are the same price as a cinema entry. The experience of an exhibition with a luxury brand is also a first approach to potential customers who would necessarily dare to enter the stores to browse and look at the clothes as they are out of reach. It becomes a first democratic access to Haute Couture: Nathalie Bondil often repeats that it is easier to see a Picasso or an impressionist painting in many museums around the world, but to see a Haute Couture dress is impossible.

Even if you are an A-list actress, a top fashion editor or a client and that you are among the happy few invited to Haute Couture shows, even sitting in the first row, you cannot see the details, the techniques and the beauty of Haute Couture up close. Some dresses take hundreds and thousands of hours in the Paris couture ateliers to be created. When you go to the shows, they stay on the catwalk for thirty seconds, one minute. People often do not know the difference between Haute Couture and prêt-à-porter.

The techniques and unique savoir-faire of Haute Couture can become ten exhibitions, as it is very rich and broad. Many designers changed Haute Couture, starting with Thierry Mugler in 1992 with his first couture collection, it was a revolution not to use only the "classic" couture techniques with precious embroideries on rubber for example; Viktor & Rolf with their conceptual fashion also invented a new form of Haute Couture, wearable art. These couturiers are artists. Gaultier, McQueen, Saint Laurent, Iris van Herpen. They have a vision, a story and stand out. When you see an Haute Couture dress you can feel the same emotion as when you see a sculpture or a painting in a museum. The debate of what is considered real art or not is very personal, and not actual anymore. If fashion is well curated, open and generous, not too sterilised, if it tells a story that is interesting and that some people can relate to, the public will understand it.

To finally answer the question, the reason we show fashion in museums is also to tell a story, a story of society, of fashion, of men, of women, of culture. Clothes are part of our lives and represent a way of communicating with each other, can be a symbol of social status or a representation of the specificity of local savoir-faire in creation and individuality.

FM: Can we train the body in order to serve fashion?

TML: We can definitely train the body to serve fashion. Just look at the corset for example, still present in many designers' collections — for many years it was considered oppressive. Gaultier and Mugler both contributed in bringing it back into contemporary fashion of the early eighties. Its use is often misunderstood as at first it was not used to constrict the waist but to lift up the body position and the shape, like military officers in the nineteenth century wore it to support their backs and give them endurance on their horses. Historically it was also used to create a shape that could correspond to the beauty standards of a time, it went through many revolutions and still exists in different forms, with waist trainers for example, and Spanx. Fashion is part fantasy and what is conveyed in magazines, in fashion shows are not the real people's bodies but those somehow dictated for years by other people defining what beauty is or was. For women, and for men.

Men's bodies in the eighties and in the early two-thousands went into a radical change from muscular beefy silhouettes to skinny. Even Karl Lagerfeld did his famous diet to make sure he could fit in Hedi Slimane's skinny clothes for Dior back then. Fashion will always have an effect on the bodies, even on politics; in the early eighties it was all about female empowerment, women working at big positions in enterprises, the athletic shape was more valued, thanks to Jane Fonda's videos, but the shoulder went to become very broad, imposing, masculine. Now it is about reality stars like Kim Kardashian and her "derrière". You see a new body shape and then fashion adapted to these new bodies.

FM: The word "intellectual" was coined at a time of extreme political anxiety. I wonder if today, more than ever before, fashion has a political role? And in which way?

TML: The role of fashion in politics is longstanding and still under debate. The spotlight is much too often now with social medias placed on a pedestal to be used as a tool to debate whether fashion is about utility, opinion or also has to do with ageism to sartorial choices. One of the best recent examples would be two first ladies, one ex, Hillary Clinton, scrutinised with her pantsuits and the other would be Brigitte Macron, also scrutinised because of her age, looks, but also length of her hair and skirts. A lot of sexist double standards exist and the politics behind is connected to the values of society. The rise of Donald Trump and the fall of Harvey Weinstein also had repercussions in fashion with many feminist collections, most notably the Dior collection of Spring 2017 by Maria Grazia Chiuri with the now cult t-shirts with the slogan "We should all be Feminists", reminding those of Katharine Hamnett, who launched this trend in the early eighties with her slogan t-shirts "Choose Life" and "Education not Missiles". Fur and animal skins became another battle with Peta in the past decades. The new ethical stance of being eco-friendly and upcycling like Viktor & Rolf did with three Haute Couture collections, using either their own archives or second-hand couture dresses, or the recent environmental footprint issue raised by designer Stella McCartney who questioned a system recycling only one per cent of the clothes it creates. The political actuality and concerns become part of the social mechanism, evaluating the role of fashion and politics together.

FM: Why do body standards change over the years while certain attributes remain as classics? What forces these changes in your

opinion? From "The Birth of Venus" (c. 1486) by Botticelli, to Marie Antoinette, Louise Brooks, Bettie Page, Twiggy, Kim Kardashian...

TML: Beauty standards and its perception vary with different cultures. A tanned body, considered healthy and a symbol of wealth in the United States or in Italy is seen as vulgar in Canada and not beautiful in Japan. The idea of perfection is different but the base stays the same. The beautiful, voluptuous women of Rubens' paintings had double chins; something that would be immediately photoshopped by any photographer nowadays. There is a pressure by society and a need to conform by many to blend in and the imagery of perfection is often transmitted via popular culture, whether they are represented in paintings or sculptures, on television and medias or in movies and television. Fashion also helps to re-evaluate the necessities and the force to change the habits by rethinking the ideals. For example Coco Chanel changed the rules with radical ideas at the time presenting clothes that were luxurious but not to the standards of femininity of her era, with looser shapes.

FM: What about the modern tribes formed by our affiliation to a certain designer?

TML: I find these very artificial. The real role of a muse has long been lost and the alleged muses now are only created with the paycheck that comes with it. Very few actresses wear designers they really like because brands offer "benefits" with wearing their designs.

Same with sitting at a fashion show's front row wearing the new handbag. It is advertising. Image. It is relayed fast on social media, something that even ten years ago we could not have thought possible. Also, the role of the designers is less focused on real talent than on their power of attraction, it is one big popularity contest. Few break the rules every seasons. By being linked to a "tribe" people choose their clans and which ones they want to identify with. Identity is key to brands and also to the spokesperson as how they want to be perceived.

The commercial landscape is uniform wherever you go in the world, everything has been globalised. It now more or less corresponds to the number of likes a celebrity has rather than the singularity, individualism of each person. I think the power of the internet to launch trends is not really genuine compared the craze triggered for example by a pop star like Madonna in the eighties when she launched a trend with her bracelets and crucifix, which was very natural, organic and was what fashion from the streets was really about. Now they have teams with strategies on how to create artificially these trends and even buy their own popularity with likes and followers that are totally artificial. The genuine ones will survive!

FM: We witness how the modern fashion model's posture has changed, the use of hands, and the choreography for the most part, is now a rather straight walking line. How would you explain this phenomenon and the reasons behind these changes, if we compare them to twenty, thirty, forty years back?

TML: The first models and fashion shows were lengthy presentations that were for wealthy clients in salons with no music and did not allow any fantasies from the models; it was pure and about the garments and their fabrics and the techniques. The models were in close relation with the couturiers, it was not the same type of relation as now where models have become anonymous after the very intense supermodel era ended in the nineties. Now shows are more important than clothes or the models; the sets are enormous, multimillion-dollars extravaganzas for 12 minutes, whether it is Chanel recreating a spaceship, a forest or an airport or supermarket at Grand Palais for their show, or Dior who will cover their walls with hundreds of thousands of real flowers for a single show.

The first fashion show to be publicised was certainly Dior in 1947 with his "New Look" collection. I think these presentations changed with the fifties' and sixties' fashion in that they became more liberated and playful and corresponded also to the music at the time, everything except static.

Thierry Mugler surely contributed to make fashion shows mainstream and popular by presenting them in arenas where tickets were sold sometimes to 6,000 people. Models like Pat Cleveland were entertainers, just like Naomi Campbell was recognised for her walk. The theatricality came with Mugler in the early eighties and has been used since by many designers, from Gaultier, Versace (think of "Freedom" by George Michael for the spring 1991 show...) and Galliano who every season used a thematic approach to their collections, which is now something untrendy. In the nineties, the industry got tired of the supermodels, these ten to twelve girls that were basically doing everything, and the music industry brought a post-punk movement, grunge, that brought a new ideal of beauty — a new revolution and mostly new standards of beauty lead by Kate Moss and newcomers like Alexander McQueen and minimalists like Helmut Lang, Martin Margiela and later Hedi Slimane, who brought new ways to present fashion which was closely linked to music.

The models' behaviour on the catwalk certainly had to do with the directions given by the couturiers, often acting like stage directors asking them to play silent movie characters on the catwalk.

FM: Today we experience a shift in the way the body is represented in general fashion, as well as through imagery. The previous decades were overly sexual, thus today the body is almost fully covered. Why in your opinion?

TML: I think that in 2017–18, a lot has changed in the representation of the body. The freedom acquired in the sixties certainly changed and will still change, for political reasons, for accommodating religions but also because of movements like #MeToo which will most probably weaken the representations of an objectified and overly sexualised submissive woman in different medias and popular culture. Women fought for their rights for decades and the Harvey Weinstein effect will certainly change the sexualisation of fashion imagery, which was followed by allegations to famous fashion photographers who saw their careers abruptly stopped as the limits of acceptance of certain behaviours were questioned and re-evaluated. In my opinion fashion shows like Victoria's Secret will disappear in a few years as even in fashion magazines and advertising, the porno chic era of Tom Ford and Carine Roitfeld is long gone and models do not relate to it as the millennial models have a different etiquette.

ANTONIO MANCINELLI

Deputy Editor of Marie Claire Italy, author and writer

BODY

FILEP MOTWARY: How connected are fashion designers today to the body they design for?

ANTONIO MANCINELLI: The attempt to carry out a valuable fashion project cannot overlook the centrality of the body, which on one hand brings back to the spotlight a dialogue with the material, and that means to be able to feel, to experience, to connect with the carnality of things, according to the philosopher Merleau-Ponty. On the other hand, the consideration for the physicality theorised by Roland Barthes is still valid, so in fashion an ideal body exists, and it's embodied by the one of the model or mannequin, a word that in French does not have a specific gender, but highlights the inorganic origin of the concept of clothing. Designers nowadays are trying to find some middle ground between these two opposites, thus moving away from the "top model" towards the "pop model": now we can see on the runways human specimens that are increasingly imperfect, coming from different ethnic groups, rounder than usual, or leaner, lankier, taller, shorter, and also more fluid in relation to the male / female gender binary concept. Personally, however, I believe that the idea still persists that, in an era of continuous changes, the body also changes, and then it becomes a "fashionable body": in other words, a body that changes according to the different seasons and to a designer's style. A meeting point that stands for the connection between the structure and the current aesthetics, but only for a limited period of time. And this is definitely not good for a fashion that, these days, lists inclusiveness among its keywords.

FM: According to Dr. Anthony Synnott's book "The Body Social" originally published in 1993, the transformations the body goes through in time also affect one's self and change it. How is the meaning of the "body" approached in fashion, considering its permanent outline and the fact that it is something generic?

AM: In fashion, the body never stops wearing a code, or being inscribed into a code. Fashion has become the new state of being in the contemporary world, and it is precisely in the postmodern age that the construction of a personal identity is perceived as the reshaping of the body, and the fully-dressed body in particular! The body has risen to a privileged object for fashion. The body has taken the place of consciousness and has become a writing surface, a living whiteboard. But things do not change if the body is naked. The naked body is always covered with ideology and aestheticism, or it is surrendered to representation and its ideology. We wear our own nakedness. The same applies to the body as an image, that changes the perception of our body and the relationship we have with it, and it leads to narcissism and to our obsession with "beautiful, supreme, immortal bodies", as Barthes used to call them. Even today, capitalist societies foster the consumption of the body with our gaze, our desire, and it's an erotic, immortal body. The myth of the youthful body created by the media is the suppression of the concepts of death and old age, and it also leads to neglecting the clothes suitable for the elderly, that are becoming increasingly irrelevant. This myth of the youthful body, according to Roland Barthes, also leads to the obsession with a slender body.

FM: About posture: our body expresses itself holding different positions depending on the conditions we put ourselves in. There is a different posture for the athlete, the soldier, the doctor, the teacher... Our body looks different when in agony, when happy or tired. In your opinion what formulated the model's posture and registered it universally as we know it?

AM: "Posturing: Photographing the Body in Fashion", an exhibition co-created by young curators / stars Shonagh Marshall and Holly Hay, deconstructs how the latest generation has freed itself of the human form. By looking at their work you could understand how today the model's posture seems to increasingly embrace an apparently "natural" dimension, while in fact it is not natural at all. It is always the result of a deliberate effort that focuses on achieving a posture that no woman could have in her everyday life. In general, this strategy also leads to a certain degree of stereotyping, as the model is clearly posing, and is therefore a reference to certain photographic conventions that have been defined in the field of fashion photography. Conventions that are typified by a fundamental unnaturalness of the model's posture compared to her natural body posture, obtained through an emphasis on the limbs instead of the breasts and the hips. The model's posture is the one of an idealised body, universal and therefore unreal, non-existent.

FM: What about the face in combination with the body?

AM: Did anyone see any happy, serene face on the latest fashion shows? Smiles were a rare sight, and only a couple of supermodels, in fact always the same ones, showed a glimmer of happiness to the audience. Nowadays this trend is getting worse, with wooden supermodels that mostly convey their own self-awareness, but also a certain anxiety for the future. Expressionless faces that do not look good even on the most beautiful girls. Perhaps their dourness has increased as a reflection of the times we live in. The models' gestures and facial expressions have changed a lot over the years, along with the different emotions, moods and lifestyles over the past decades. In the sixties, at the time of Veruschka and Twiggy's success, affected and theatrical gestures were all the rage. The seventies introduced a certain defiance of social conventions. During those years the models, rebellious and mischievous, used to look straight into the eyes of the audience during the fashion shows, and they all had a no-nonsense, resolute walk. Then in the eighties the supermodels started to smile, wiggling their hips and being ironically aggressive, they became the symbol of a wild age, they almost danced towards the exit. The blank stare only began in the nineties.

FM: Humans have been working on reconstructing the body and proportion through clothing... Why this particular need?

AM: The system for fashion and cosmetics sales reveals the high amount of expectations that exist on the female body, and because of these it also becomes the subject for transformative projects. The objectification of the body implies that the body is closely related to the society itself, where this body is placed and on which it inscribes certain meanings. In this regard, the male or female body is analysed from a social point of view, that makes it an ideal setting for recognition and differentiation. Considering that the social recognition of the body entails its symbolic fragmentation, it's the media that represent the reliable tool for this symbolic construction. In this respect, the individual is socially defined through his corresponding conformity to certain images and cultural codes, and this process contributes to assigning a precise social role and a well-defined identity.

FM: Could we suggest clothing is a living organism?

AM: Fashion is a living and dynamic organism. It must be, because its task is to adhere to, and sometimes to form or even anticipate changes in society. In the influential essay "Fashion: A Philosophy" by Lars Fr. H. Svendsen, the principle of fashion initially lay in a "substitutive logic", driven by an innovating compulsion, aimed at the perennial creation of something new ("The principle of fashion demanded an increasingly fast cycle, it required any object to become irrelevant as quickly as possible in order to be able to introduce a new one".) Nowadays the dictates have changed, and this process has been replaced by a "supplementary logic", according to which "all trends are reusable and a new fashion is not meant to replace the previous ones: it settles for adding to them." The author has one final observation: fashion is nothing more than a "journey through the inconvenient truths of the world?" But now the question becomes: "What truths?" Svendsen answers: "That we pursue the ephemeral, that we live in an increasingly fictitious reality, that our identity is becoming less and less permanent? If so, then fashion is revealing us truths while also being the most active driving force in their creation".

FM: In the end, what does clothing serve today?

AM: Our focus should shift towards consumers and their need to assert their identity through their purchase of symbolic values, such as designer clothes. That's the essence of fashion, to produce effective signs, and yet in a short time those signs will become ineffective; thus the symbolic value sought by the consumer "is consumed faster and faster" and the true object of his/her desires therefore becomes the search for the satisfaction of new needs, perpetually created by fashion. About the relationship between fashion and the body, above all we should emphasise that fashion always enjoyed a certain freedom compared to the actual shape of the body; on the contrary, it is the body, or rather our perception of the human body that was always affected by the current trends, a quite meaningful concept, because it's aiming to prove how it's the body that is trying to adapt to fashion, always striving for an everlasting ideal of beauty, and for this reason always being deeply dissatisfied, inevitably.

FM: What about modern society? Are we connected to the clothes we choose to wear? Do we seek for a deeper meaning into clothing?

AM: Two social moving forces become essential to understand fashion nowadays: the big companies and the consumers, because commercial interests and the drive to set ourselves apart from our peers — both by designers who want to introduce innovative products, and also by the wide range of consumers that have different tastes — make the dynamics of fashion highly complex. In addition to this, there is also the role played by media culture in fostering a looser kind of self-awareness, which is also mirrored by some more individualised or niche choices of attire. Consumption, significance, spaces and production must be taken into consideration in their mutual relationship in order to better understand all the various cultural expressions, including fashion, of course.

FM: Why is the oppression of the body always present in fashion?

AM: The oppression of the body by fashion is a concept strictly limited to the Western fashion system, which is still trapped by the sizing system, compared to clothing of Eastern or African origin, for example. I want to pay tribute to Susan Bordo, the feminist writer who in her essay "Unbearable Weight: Feminism, Western Culture, and the Body" published in 1993 expounded a quite interesting theory about the spreading of female eating disorders in the contemporary society, focusing the debate on the connection between food problems and the exposure of women to various social and communicative agents of a certain type of body and identity. Bordo insists on the parallelism between adaptability and body shaping, eating disorders and surgery.

According to Bordo, it is almost like we are facing a pathology caused by fashion with its imposition of models and its crystallisation into external identities. A classic example is the corset, fashionable in the nineteenth century and worn exclusively by women, that was in itself an imposition through clothing and was therefore an expression of movement restriction and a way of behavioural control at the social level.

EMOTION

FM: How can we overcome ourselves through dressing while avoiding obsolescence?

AM: Fashion can be examined in many ways: from a psychological point of view it is a non-verbal tool that we use to communicate. On a sociological level it marks different ages and decades, but on an individual level it allows us to identify ourselves within a group or to define ourselves through a personal style. Fashion communicates identity elements that refer to both social and personal characteristics. The uniform is an excellent example of how clothing can tell the people around us that we belong to a specific social group, but at the same time it is capable of eluding the planned obsolescence of an industry that is releasing too many products and too often. On a personal level, the style we develop over time is a way to define ourselves and make ourselves identifiable to others.

FM: How long does it take for a model to be 100 per cent conscious of what she/he is wearing in the current state of fashion? (In comparison with the eighties and nineties before social media and dependency on any gadgets as such existed). What determines if something is surprising or emotional enough on the catwalk?

AM: I believe the difference is in the possibility of talking through social media, thus overcoming that silent presence status that typified the role of models in the eighties and nineties. Although, when I interviewed Olivier Saillard for his "Models Never Talk" performance, he told me that between supermodels and the designers who picked them a special kind of alchemy burgeoned, and that is the reason why Saillard had decided to make them talk. Thanks to social networks today there are models that can and actually do want to talk — a perfect example is Adwoa Aboah, who is half Ghanaian, half English, an actress, a model, an activist and recently also a lawyer who, through her Instagram, is able to make real statements; another example is the choice for the catwalk of personalities coming from the transgender world, such as Hari Nef or Andreja Pejić, who is able to speak of herself as a "gender-fluid" person. This certainly speeds up and enhances their role as influencers in society not just on an aesthetical level, but also on a cultural and social level: and it seems to me that many of them are using clothes as an integral part of their self-expression, a kind of conscious self-representation. And their presence is increasingly connected to the message that brands want to communicate to their consumers.

FM: Can we manoeuvre emotion through fashion?

AM: Unfortunately, I must admit that the answer is, even today, affirmative. Clothes and accessories are the link between our deepest inner self and our outward appearance. They are not just the expression of the latest fashion trends, but also of the profound relationship we have with ourselves and with others, with the person we are (our real self), or who we would like to be (ideal self), or who we think we should be (imposed self). According to the social psychologist Marc-Alain Descamps fashion is a "complex psychosocial phenomenon [...] An imitative infection that includes numerous vectors, each corresponding to one of the domains of our society". According to this author, in order to understand fashion, "the social dimension far surpasses the personal psychological dimension: every dress or suit is a uniform, that makes sense only in relation to a certain group".

FM: How does emotion interfere with your role as a fashion journalist?

AM: Whenever I go to see a show I try to mentally reset all my expectations, my desires and, why not, even my preferences for one brand or another. My hope is to come and be able to see any collection with a fresh outlook, with no preconceptions that I may have developed after seeing the previous collection. But I'm still human, and so the emotion that fashion can provoke always has to do with all the different elements which are part of a show: most of all the storytelling of an inner world that belongs to a certain designer in a specific way and that expresses itself through his clothes, but also the soundtrack, the staging, the casting of the models... In some way what moves me is the union between a personal story and the due opportunity to make the goods shown at that moment commercially enticing. Fashion always inspires me emotions, paradoxically, even when, in addition to the emotional element, there is also a technical aspect, bound to the search for some kind of formal and handcrafted perfection. In one word, the only emotion that interferes with my work as a fashion journalist is: authenticity. And originality.

FM: Why is the ceremonial process of dressing linked with achieving a higher state of feelings? Can we read humans through clothing?

AM: Clothing belongs, in all respects, to non-verbal communication. From a psychological point of view, the way a person is dressed is also information about his personality: there is no diagnostic and psychological relationship missing from the first few lines to describe a person for what he/she looks like, if he/she is well-groomed and is able to take good care of his/her appearance or not. Appearance is an open window on our inner self: sometimes it reflects how we are, sometimes how we want to be, sometimes even that we are forced to play a role we don't enjoy. Many people, after a life-changing experience, such as getting a new job or a promotion, or maybe a divorce or an engagement, totally change their looks, their clothing, and their dress style. I'm thinking of Rose McGowan's haircut after the #MeToo movement started and the publication of her autobiography "Brave", just to make an example. And so, the ritual of clothing is highly metaphorical: as a daily ritual of dressing and undressing our body, as a sign linked to certain moments of the day or to certain rites of passage, such as a marriage or any kind of ceremony, our clothes become a metaphor that can interpret different kinds of experience.

FM: Why do we exhibit fashion in museums, apart from the financial and historical reasons?

AM: An exhibition should not be just informative or educational, but also inspiring to arouse a reaction in its audience. I will also say, in the words of Maria Luisa Frisa, director of the degree course in Fashion Design and Multimedia Arts at IUAV in Venice, that "a fashion show holds different dimensions together: historical research, phantasmagorical display, targeted communication. By itself, it's a mirror of fashion complexity which straddles many areas: the academy and the shop, the pages of a magazine and the body." ("la Repubblica", March 31, 2017).

FM: At which point fashion makes us feel vulnerable? How does it comment about the way we live?

AM: "There is more reason in your body than in your deepest philosophy", wrote Nietzsche. And today more than ever, in an era of thriving appearances and an ever-decreasing faith in religions, fashion, as a carrier of meanings, makes us more permeable and therefore more vulnerable. The body becomes a glorious instance, an ideological sanctuary in which the individual consumes the last remnants of his alienation. I speak of "alienation" because nowadays we no longer "live" our body, but, just like schizophrenics, we perceive it as something outside ourselves, as something we must "reshape" to make it as close as possible to all the canons of health, strength, beauty that our culture advertise so that we can be accepted and we are able to accept ourselves. We no longer see the body as a "carrier", but instead as an "obstacle" to living in the world, if it does not correspond to the criteria set by fashion to be admired, craved for and desired.

POLITICS

FM: What is so important about being new? Does creation have to be new?

AM: Fashion must be modern, by its design. In the Italian language, the word "fashion" ["moda"] has the same root as the word "modern". In its broadest sense it seems to be the key element in the shaping of what we call the "spirit of the times", or Zeitgeist. Even when the "new" feeds on what we have already seen, it is still a change of direction compared to the past period, it is a novelty. Of course, when we look at a garment, we also immediately identify its era; a hat or a pair of shoes are able to explain the world to us more clearly than certain literary works. And this occurs also when it evokes periods of strong conservatism, such as the one we are experiencing today. And it binds deeply to those categories, as Lars Fr. H. Svendsen called them, of the "new" and "change". This sheds light on some aspects of living in today's world and on the choices (or lack thereof) that our existence has to face. Moreover, Walter Benjamin defined fashion as an "endless recurrence of the new" and according to Thomas Carlyle the original purpose of clothing is not the basic need to keep ourselves warm or the decency, but the embellishment. The clothes are therefore "the key to the interpretation of the world" and this will only work if our outward appearance is mirroring our inner self.

FM: How is fashion revelatory of the social mechanism and politics?

AM: Fashion is able to reveal and anticipate social and political mechanisms by making social developments evident. By its very nature, it must constantly confront issues such as gender, wealth, the construction of our identity, but also the desires, the dreams and the interactions of entire generations. Actually, it is not just fashion, but the way it is used: for example, if a classic style is chosen by both Michelle Obama and Melania Trump, the results are totally opposite. Michelle has most of her clothes designed exclusively by American designers or by members of minority ethnic groups (Jason Wu, Altuzarra), while Melania wears mostly clothes made by Europeans and in particular by Italian designers, such as Dolce & Gabbana. While the former first lady, with her appearance, is saying "I am one of you", the latter says "I am not like you, and I have no intention of becoming one of you". Meanwhile, Maria Grazia Chiuri has made feminism the key feature of her Dior line, and in order to prepare for her first show she had read "Women Who Run With the Wolves", the classic essay of pop feminism published in 1992. As for the clothes of subcultural groups, from African Americans to the queer world or the working class, they used fashion as a gesture of political affirmation. Today, the societies where it is more interesting to "use" fashion as the key to interpreting the current moment in history are those where Islam is the dominant culture. As Elizabeth Bucar explained in "The Atlantic", in her article "How Muslim Women Use Fashion To Exert Political Influence. The rebellious potential of an apparently conservative style".

FM: What about the way it is formed today? Who is directing it?

AM: Money. Earnings. Profits. Revenues. Through fashion we can analyse an entire society because it is a living entity and also a witness to the economic, behavioural and cultural life for all ages. As Coco Chanel used to say, "Fashion is not something that exists in dresses only. Fashion is in the sky, in the street, fashion has to do with ideas, the way we live, what is happening". Its connection with economics stems from the fact that fashion is a real business contributing to fuel the economy of a country such as Italy, with a massive turnover of more than one hundred and seventy thousand billion euros. Marketing plays a fundamental role since it gives any product its own personality, making the purchase a unique experience. It starts from a careful analysis of the consumer needs and then proceeds to elaborate every aspect of the matter, such as pricing, production, distribution, but also never losing sight of the central role that emotions and feelings play in the fashion system. Marketing then combines economic and management aspects with the emotional requirements that characterise fashion, thus becoming vital for it.

FM: Philosopher Edmund Husserl believed that the body can be viewed from two different perspectives: first from the outside, as a solid physical object and secondly, through the sensations it carries within, the living body. Based on these two descriptions how does the fashion industry perceive the body?

AM: The fashion industry, by mostly working on large-scale production, can only think of a generic, ideal, universal body. At the same time, however, it cannot help but remind us the Husserlian difference between a "me-world" and a "me-body". Hence the fundamental distinction between the living body or one's own body (Leib) and the body as an object (Körper), on whose phenomenological evidences are based respectively human and historical sciences (which phenomenology lastingly influenced, beginning with psychology) and natural sciences. For Merleau-Ponty, in his "Phenomenology of Perception", 1945, the original foundation of experience is not pure consciousness, but the perceptive body as an undauntedly ambiguous phenomenon in its essence as a reflection of the world, formed by the same "flesh of the world". Consciousness — as Sartre used to say — is always "in situation", that is defined by its physical, social and historical limits, as well as by the reciprocal relationship with the living bodies of other men; at the same time, however, it is a constant ambition for liberation, albeit conditioned, which seeks new possible horizons of meaning.

FM: Not more than twenty years ago, designers such as McQueen and John Galliano were creating entire collections inspired by tribes, global historical references, and folklore. Today this approach is considered as inappropriate.

AM: Unfortunately, the debate on cultural appropriation, for me as an Italian, is quite difficult to understand. Some argue that the adoption or use of elements of a subculture by the members of a dominant culture would be disrespectful and would constitute a form of oppression and dispossession. I do not know about this: Italians are crossbreed by nature, because of our history and traditions, and wherever we go, we tend to integrate into the social fabric. However, for us it is always a matter of spontaneous migration: we move to other countries, by legal or illicit means, looking for a better future. In this context it becomes difficult for us to understand why for white American boys to intertwine their hair in cornrows — which is mostly typical of African Americans — has become an offensive gesture rather than a stylistic decision. A progressive white American would not allow his sons to cut their hair like our Serie A footballers: the mohawk haircut is considered the heritage of Native Americans, and among their tribes it established the identity of their leaders and protectors. Here we tend to identify it with Radja Nainggolan, a very popular football player. The question is: if for Americans to cut their hair according to the custom of a population they oppressed for centuries and pushed to the verge of extinction is not recommended, what do Americans think when they come to Italy and see Balotelli's hairstyle? How many degrees of appropriation and re-appropriation are necessary for a sign to lose its original meaning, or to gain a new one in a different context?

FM: What happened in between?

AM: The debate on cultural appropriation has now spread far beyond the academic circles in which it was born; a decisive push came with the call into question of pop music and fashion. The opening of the Dapper Dan boutique in partnership with Gucci reignites the debate on cultural appropriation. On the threshold between inspiration and robbery, between hybridisation and cynicism, fashion, like other areas of the creative industry, is increasingly facing factors that damage the originality and the authenticity of its stylistic offer: it's both a challenge and an opportunity to redefine the creative processes on which collections are based. Fashion has always been influenced by different cultures and subcultures, and often reinterpreted them to create something new: while Vivienne Westwood in England brought punk on the catwalk in the late seventies, at the same time Siouxsie Sioux (who started in the punk scene) sang "Hong Kong Garden" and made abundant use of Sino-Japanese iconography, with no claim of oriental origin or any anthropological intent, just an aesthetic one.

FM: What are the dynamics of a fashion tribe?

AM: The real tribes, or the ones with a lifestyle that makes them identifiable, are coming back. Because, as Clive Martin — star of British lifestyle journalism ("The Guardian", "Vice Magazine") — said, we need tribes to reinvent ourselves. Please give them back to us, it's a matter of principle: boys and girls have been silenced by a cultural and economic system that no longer has any creative and original thoughts. For instance, today I may have a Neohippy-Occupy vibe but tomorrow, maybe, I will be Haul Boy, a vlogger who shows off on YouTube his consumerist haul of clothes and cosmetics. Or maybe I can be both things at the same time... Fashion is mourning the global and international subcultures of the past, when it was easy to trace their historical origin, or a mythical place, an icon, or an anthem. Today the tribes are no longer born spontaneously; they just take off because of an influencer, or a stylist, or Tumblr. They have an overly specific origin, they tend to honour the uniqueness of a single person. This is why tribes today seem to be so difficult to identify, so ephemeral. But we must keep an eye on them, because on the web, and not only there, authenticity has become the rarest and most precious commodity. Authenticity, which is the opposite of speed, tends to hide, to slip away.

FM: At what level are we conscious of what we see, buy or wear? Does it matter?

AM: It definitely matters, of course it matters! According to Gayatri Chakravorty Spivak, fashion is the expression where the narratives of the transnational capitalist domain get formed (Gayatri Chakravorty Spivak, "Critica della ragione postcoloniale. Verso una storia del presente in dissolvenza", Milan: Meltemi, 2004, p. I24). But fashion is also ambivalent: it is able to convey stories, to set up spaces, to produce myths, to give voice to the senses but it is also a conflict area, just like the contemporary global world is a complex scenario, in which clothing codes can communicate and move "from the sidewalk to the catwalk": the places of everyday culture today are able to define fashions even before our stylistic research can elaborate a luxury goods code for its products. It is a lesson that casualwear multinationals have learned all too well, and because of it they were able to formulate some misrepresentations like, for example, since the late eighties at least, they have built their values and mythologies drawing parasitically from the styles and tastes of young people living in the Western main cities.

SUZY MENKES

Vogue International Editor

BODY

FILEP MOTWARY: In 1969, you released a book titled "How to be a model" with Twiggy on the cover. Ms Menkes, I wonder what did it take to be a model then compared to now and how the meaning of the term shifted from the seventies?

SUZY MENKES: In the seventies becoming a model was something new because the idea of a very young woman, still in her teens, was alien to what had happened right through the fifties and the early sixties. Then the magazines featured women in their twenties who were photographed in grand poses. That was how magazines presented fashion images.

Twiggy was indicative of a dramatic change in the sixties. The idea of this very young woman was new then. But today we are actually trying to escape from that idea of super-young models and to think that it would be better if they were 18 or over and more womanly.

The invention of the contraceptive pill in the sixties made everything so different. The idea of Twiggy in a mini skirt was quite provocative but in a fresh way. She was indicative of the model of the time.

In a later period, Kate Moss was emblematic of the woman of the nineties. But I don't think that being a model was so completely different to the end of the sixties. It's a question of history and change.

FM: How long does it take for a model to be 100 per cent conscious of what she/he is wearing, how would the body serve these clothes best (in terms of ways presenting them) in the current state of fashion?

SM: The idea that time is a luxury applies to every part of our lives. I don't think it necessarily applies to a model on a shoot because in that case it can take a long time to put on the make-up, to get everything together. The actual shoot might not take long but the preparation takes ages. But thinking of the speed with which the models change during runway shows, they are incredibly rapid and seem to get faster and faster...

The bad period was when models became so young and waif-like. I would put that down to the nineties because certainly in the eighties the supermodels had strong bodies. Many of those models, like Naomi Campbell, are still around and they always represented something bolder than a little waif.

Kate Moss in the nineties changed the shape and the look. Other things came with that, for example, the vision of Gucci and how Tom Ford presented models in advertisements in the late nineties and early two-thousands. It was a sexualizing of fashion, on the runway and particularly in the Gucci advertising campaigns.

Yet, I don't think this focus on the body applied to all models. Now there is much more diversity with different model agencies and so many models from all over the world. The idea that every model has to be skinny, I just think that's wrong!

FM: Is there room for the body to be appreciated as a totem in fashion as it was in the fifties through the "New Look" let's say?

SM: You cannot say today that there is only one type of model. For example: last year when I went to South Korea and also to Japan, there was no doubt that the Asian outlines for male and female models were much closer, in terms of silhouette that in European countries. That is why the clothes seem to be able to morph from male to female without making any great statement. This is completely different in America, for example, where both men and women are physically bigger and also have very different shapes.

Especially in South Korea, I remember vividly that there was a feeling of the absorption of one sex into another and that is very much of our time. I don't think you have to go to South Korea to see that now. You can see it in the fashion shows of today.

FM: How connected are fashion designers today to the body they design for?

SM: It's a different world now. With the passing of Azzedine Alaïa, it is a good time to view and to realise how relatively few fashion designers of today follow the anatomy of the female body when they design. This was absolutely Alaïa's line, which was to make garments, mostly dresses that curve around the body of a woman. That was their appeal and also their brilliance because it is not easy to follow the female silhouette, which requires advanced cutting and draping.

I saw Azzedine Alaïa at work many times. He, personally, worked out the shape, drew the garment, and cut the paper in sizes. That would then be sent off to Italy to a company that turned his flat designs into rounded knitwear. This was one particular designer, who, compared to Rei Kawakubo of Comme des Garçons was exactly the opposite. I cannot remember any clothes that she did that were very close to the body but at the same time they created an extraordinary line.

Designers do different things. In our current age of diversity, I don't think there should be the idea that there is only one style of woman, as it was in the fifties with curvy bust lines, slim waists, gentle hips, and always high heels. I don't think that look suits every woman — to have a variety is the ideal in the modern world.

FM: How connected is society to the clothes they choose to wear? Do we seek for a deeper meaning into clothing?

SM: I don't think that the majority of people are seeking deep meaning. The majority of most women — and men as well — want clothes that move with the body. We are past the era when women were in tiptoes with pin-high heels or where men stuffed themselves into huge waistcoats in order to look smart. People have gone beyond that.

Semi-sports clothes for women have changed everything. It is now perfectly normal to go to the office in stretch trousers and sneakers. If you go now into the subways of any city from the Far East, through America, India, Europe — everywhere people wear sneakers because they are comfortable. Sports shoes allow you to use your energy as you want to, they don't slow you down and they have also become status pieces. Even Haute Couture designers like Karl Lagerfeld at Chanel have shown sneakers, while in the past people would have worn them only on the tennis court.

Now, sports shoes are decorated and given signals of all kinds. They have become cool property and people love to wear them. All that is something I would say happened in the last seven years, maybe even less. In this case we are not talking about a deeper meaning, but about people who feel that it gives them an identity to wear the kind of shoes that rappers or sports stars wear.

When we talk about deeper meaning in clothes — that might mean in the past people wearing black clothes to mark a death in their family. Queen Victoria wore black after her husband died for the rest of her life.

I cannot think really anything like that today, that sends out a message to everybody else. Certainly though, there are types of clothing that express certain characteristics. Prada is an example of that: the real followers of Prada aim to say: "Like Miuccia Prada, I appreciate the artistic side of the world." But few look for this depth in what they wear. The majority seeks mostly comfort.

EMOTION

FM: How does emotion clash with your role as a fashion critic? Is there a possibility to be emotionally moved by a show while the clothes are less moving?

SM: I was trained as a fashion editor for newsprint. I never really thought I was going to wear any of these clothes and so I was quite objective. If you ask anybody who is involved in fashion, those who worked in the periods as I did, everyone picks out the same shows as the ones that really moved them, when they felt involved or excited. I don't think it is a very personal thing.

Of course, personally I would prefer to wear Issey Miyake than I would wear Chanel but I have never really put that in the equation of when I am judging a fashion show. It is not about me, it is about the quality of what I am seeing.

FM: Why is the ceremonial process of dressing linked with achieving a higher state of feelings?

SM: I don't know about emotion, I think that the emotion tends to be more about the occasion a garment is worn for. People feel very emotional about something they wore at an emotional moment — for example, a woman who met the man she later married would remember and tell you what she was wearing that time. I think that the greatest emotion people get out of clothes is pleasure — feeling good, or maybe feeling comfortable.

FM: But we did experience shows that were more emotional than others like with John Galliano or with Yohji Yamamoto.
How difficult is for emotion to engage with the current state of the fashion industry and why?

SM: I think it is a mistake to remember every single John Galliano show and every single McQueen show as something immensely moving and exceptional. There were some shows that were good but not great and there were a few shows — that we all remember — that were absolutely extraordinary and exceptional. But who says there are not more to come? They didn't all appear at once and they didn't all necessarily carry on producing exceptional things — I do not think we should rule out now the idea of a show that makes us feel moved or excited. Why imagine that it's all over?"

POLITICS

FM: How is fashion revelatory of the social mechanism and politics?

SM: Everybody, to a certain extent, dresses for their working lives in a way that they think appropriate for their job. Therefore, they are revealing how they see themselves, not necessarily how others see them.

It is interesting that the current Prime Minister of England (Theresa May), since the beginning of the time when she took over, always wore fancy shoes with very plain clothes. I have noticed that recently she just stopped fancy shoes, I don't know if she has come to a conclusion that life is too serious, but obviously, this was a decision that she made.

With Mrs Merkel I think she is more of the idea of: "I get on with my job, I don't want to say I am a great "woman" politician in Germany. I work in clothes that are comfortable for me and my clothes mean business and that's how I dress".

I don't think it's more of a statement than that and I actually admire the way that she hasn't made any effort to get into the fashion arena.

FM: Not more than twenty years ago, designers such as Alexander McQueen and John Galliano were creating entire collections inspired by tribes, global historical references, and folklore. Today this approach is considered as inappropriate. What happened in between?

SM: It goes further back than that. I think of Yves Saint Laurent doing collections that were inspired by the Russians, dipping so deeply into foreign cultures and then making it his own. Of course his clothes may have seemed more harmonious than what was produced by Alexander McQueen, but there is still this tremendously deep creative feeling about another and quite alien culture that was used for fashion.

There was an era when Central Saint Martins was in a particular position and therefore everybody was pushed to extremes.

It is obvious to all of us now that there was this transition period with the big-name brands when they had to be shaken up for a completely new vision in order to reach the next generations. Mothers and grandmothers who had worn Christian Dior would have been absolutely flabbergasted to see what John Galliano came up with.

There always has to be, particularly now, something that is shocking. When these shocking periods come, they are followed by a period of calm-down and then I am sure there will be another one. I don't think it's all over.

We can go further back and realise how unbelievably shocking it was in the twenties to an older generation that young women cut off their hair for the very first time in hundreds of years; or how they wore skirts to reveal their knees. These things were absolutely shocking in that time and then it calmed down. You get these waves of shock followed by a much calmer period.

VIOLETA SANCHEZ

Performer

BODY

FILEP MOTWARY: How is the meaning of the "body" approached in fashion, considering its permanent outline and the fact that it is something generic?

VIOLETA SANCHEZ: Back then, there was a real friendship with the designer, not for all the models as there were those who arrived only a couple of days before each show and they had body types that were quite generic, very similar to the girls we see today but more of a size 36 minimum. There were also those of us who would inspire the designers: they liked our body, our shoulders, our proportions… The ideal body at the time was with broad shoulders, not too much bust or too much hips; a rounded butt would work perfectly OK, nice legs… good proportions in general. There was also a very close relationship between the generic body of the model with its slight differences that made it special or particularly inspiring and the production of the clothes, something that I am not sure is still the case today.

These days, clothes are almost like computer made, it's like there's the design and then a studio that usually makes it and then it's computerised and the incarnation of the clothes only comes practically at the moment of the fitting, just the day before the show. It seems that it doesn't matter at all — of course when these clothes come back from wherever they are made they are tried and fitted on a house model, something that was also the same at my time, but today it seems to have been reduced to minimum in most cases, the muse seems to have vanished.

FM: What about the technological body, the body that is dressed by computerised clothing? Why does the body still need to look and act human?

VS: Simply because it's people that are going to wear the clothes, they need to have a function: to cover your body at different stages of the seasons, the temperature, the occasion, etc. You want it more or less adorned and besides being comfortable they often need to compensate for flaws, proportions that one doesn't like… so clothes have all these functions and at the same time should be wearable. Perhaps clothes can change in the future but how are we going to interact with us and between one another? It's true that they have considerably evolved in many and different ways from not constrictive at all to extremely constrictive, loose and constrictive again, then to generic shapeless deluxe branded sport gone streetwear… Sportswomen and men, rappers, professional "people" are the new super models.

The base is the body. I also feel that although the body is going to disappear more and more in the future, the clothes will still be resting on the shoulders. They will have to contain the proportions of the body in them. What I am trying to say is that we are moving more and more towards a world that will be more of the mind or the mindless. In any case the mindless will be blobs in front of their screens, they will weight 300 kg, will be unable to move and full of ailments. For the rest maybe it will be a time for clothes that will not have functionality as priority because anyhow there will be not be many functions to be accomplished with the body anymore. We will probably walk much less; do much less things than we do now, that machines will be doing for us.

You know. What comes to mind is the White Drama collection by Comme des Garçons (Spring Summer 2012).

At the time, Olivier [Saillard] did something poetic and clever when he presented it at the Cité de la mode et du design in Paris in sterile bubbles, something I thought was very visionary. They were very beautiful silhouettes for people that didn't need to move around. They were a romantic vision of extraterrestrial beings.

FM: Should our physical structure and body outline serve an important factor to the decision whether we should follow fashion or not?

VS: Yes, of course! First of all, following fashion to me is something that should be extremely subtle in the sense that I live in France, a country where fashion is made and followed individually a lot. For instance, there is a difference between an American woman that would buy a total look and a French woman who would never buy a total look. It would not even cross her mind!

The most "total" she ever went and that's been going for a long time is the "tailleur", a jacket and a skirt or pants, other than that, the French woman mixes her clothes. I remember at the Maison de Couture Yves Saint Laurent the vendeuses who managed their clients' YSL wardrobe, while selling a piece of the season, made suggestions like "Oh but this tailleur you can also wear with the blouse from the tailleur you got three seasons ago." It was a natural thing!

Olivier Châtenet did something that I found extremely beautiful and inspiring: he has an incredible collection of vintage garments by Yves Saint Laurent and he curated a show where he dressed mannequins in mixed collections, not only by seasons but also by years. You would have a top from the summer of 1987 with a winter skirt of 1979 and so on. There was no question that all these clothes came from the same designer; you could see YSL's DNA, his vision, his gaze on the female body, his perception! And they all worked timelessly together in spite of the time and season gaps between them, in a very modern way, for some of them almost sixty years after their creation.

The body should not adjust to fashion, whatever body that is. There have been so many unfortunate fashion moments in the contemporary years like with the leggings or the low waist jeans, that every single woman was wearing at some point — it was very unfortunate. These clothes did not do any favours to them but they wore them anyhow, in a twisted "Because I am worth it" sort of way.

FM: How did your body affect or defect of you being the final choice during a casting?

VS: My case was a body that was too small and too skinny! Especially for the ready-to-wear, where clothes would arrive in generic sizes (that were much bigger than now, much, much bigger).

The generic size in ready-to-wear then was 38/36, now it is 34 maximum and the girls were around 174/176 cm, I was 172 cm and 34.

I sort of tricked my way into the clothes and when the designers liked me they would help me do that: they would roll the skirt a little bit, pin the clothes especially and just for the show. What truly served me was my sense of drama and my way to express in the clothes I was wearing on the catwalk.

When the supermodels of the nineties appeared, it was something that attracted a lot of attention on the brands that used them but this in the end also led into making them more important than the designers themselves.

The supermodels faded out after five-six years and were replaced by a new generation of models from the East, the "waif" very beautiful girls who had learned to walk from what they could watch on TV, in a very mechanical way.

They arrived like little horses with this very weird walk that everyone loved!

These beautiful tall girls were totally unknown, totally submissive; they would do exactly what they were told to, and there were zillions of them arriving, while one girl was more beautiful than the other.

When they realised how they would be used, they just continued playing their part, and they appeared like ghosts, zombified versions of what models used to be. The robot thing came gradually, these ghosts would no longer swing their hips, they would not use their hands anymore, their torso had to bend backward a certain way. Their gaze remained fixed above the head of the spectator, their eyes should never meet, no eye contact. The 90-degree angle-turn appeared, no sway in it, just a rotation, no stop and then walk backstage. The new models would not open a jacket, or take it off while walking.

This has again now changed a little bit in the sense that you will see a "hand in a pocket" but the hand is put there before the girl walks out on stage and it stays there for as long she is on the catwalk. No personal initiative yet, no interpretation, individuality to a minimum just to make it less dull, but the hips are a bit looser, the body has regained a fraction of naturality, it is coming back to life. On the runway everything now appears to be like a "lookbook" photograph, not even an inspiring photograph, you look at it quickly for purely information purposes, the shows last eight to ten minutes. The girls now are walking "lookbooks" and it's depressing.

Let's say that the models of the eighties had very strong personalities, with the models of the nineties perhaps runway personality and skill did not matter as much, but they replaced the actresses that were not glamorous at the time. We were into this anti-hero new situation where the actresses were girls next door, etc....

FM: Why do body standards change over the years while certain attributes remain as classics?

VS: It's due to the industry, it's the alimentation lobbies and what they feed us people with. This deformation of the mass body and how its opposite is simultaneously presented in the magazines as an example of how we should look, is very perverse. We are fed with sugar and salt and things that make us have no control of our bodies now. When I was in school, if there was someone who was a bit overweight, he or she was originality in that sense. Today, one child out of five are overweight in France!

Focusing on the fashion media, they propose something that is entirely unattainable as opposed to the way of life we are forced to live. When magazines started to exist, the bodies that were proposed were those that one could achieve and they were totally related to the population.

Today's suggestions are not pragmatic at all, plus we have all these new problems like bulimia or anorexia to deal with, all this dimorphic surgically modified breasts, butts impossible to fit in anything but skin-tight spandex meant to reveal the investment/statement to its full. All these of course are linked to this anxiety problems our society has. The fashion industry today is not so much content with clothes, it's much more content with accessories that everyone "can buy". You can have any type of body and still wear shoes that have a generic size, bags and sunglasses, all those things and "can-buy" items that the fashion industry is interested in are selling more than anything else. The clothes are totally peripheral, they are made only for red carpets and the front row at fashion shows, they are meant for this type of exposure. There are now red carpets everywhere and all the time, that serve the advertisement purposes of the brands for a price.

We hardly see anyone wearing Dior, Chanel or YSL for real, except on the red carpet. But there is a lot of streetwear combined with their accessories.

I remember at the time of Galliano sometimes going to the shop to have a look; there was not one single item that you could buy. Where would you wear something like that?

Now in Paris for example, they are trying to transform rue des Archives (in Le Marais, a petit-bourgeois neighbourhood next to a popular not trendy department store, Le BHV) with a mix of Avenue Montaigne and cheaper brands trying to appeal to the strongly present gay population in the area, but these shops are empty all the time.

The fashion industry changed the body when it got liberated from the corset, but as it moves in circles we then had the corset coming back and so on.

With these parallel tendencies, the Japanese and then the Belgians introduced this more visionary and intellectual way of seeing things, they went back to the shape of the body through iconic and constructive or deconstructive approaches, that was interesting, lines were moved there.

When you make an effort to dress, and personally I do and love to change my style all the time, and I guess that comes from doing it for a living; every time I go out it is an opportunity for a new disguise, a different armour.

Today our world suffers from the loss of extravagance in the way we dress. We have gone through the destructive moment, the streetwear moment and now people feel too self-conscious when they dress.

You've got to fit in a square even if you are a circle.

I have two daughters that I am trying to raise properly for instance, it's been a long fight to teach them how to eat properly at the table, to hold their bodies, to have certain gestures in their communication with the rest of the world, of grace and good manners, etc. because almost nobody does anymore. I also tried to show them through vintage and even the very cheap brands they can afford, the importance of quality in the fabric and the making, the care one should have for oneself and one's appearance that does not depend on the money you spend but on the choices you make. Beautiful things need maintenance to remain beautiful!

FM: How connected are fashion designers today to the body they design for? At the end, what does clothing serve today?

VS: I don't think they are connected. This has been lost because the streetwear thing has erased a lot of the elements in the sense that if you wear a large t-shirt and a pair of baggy jeans it doesn't matter if you have a nice or big butt, hips, boobs or a waist and so it's almost as if you don't matter. For example, one of my two daughters is quite fashion/clothes conscious. She started wearing belts, none of her friends does, the simple fact to wear a belt at 19 is a fashion statement. It seems like the new generations are a bit embarrassed, even ashamed of their bodies in spite of all the exhibitionism and pornography, or perhaps because of... As the presence of the muse almost disappeared, the body got lost in translation, and the designers now float in a disembodied ether drifting from one brand to the other. Or so it seems but maybe I am wrong...

Being comfortable as we understand it now used to be a secondary preoccupation in fashion. You could be elegant, sexy, bodies were held a different way. Today it's more about being the brand; you need to be recognised for wearing this or that. The body is almost unimportant.

FM: You worked closely with some of fashion's contemporary masters like YSL and Mugler. How different was their approach to the body if we compare the two and how is this compared as well with today's designers?

VS: Part of what is missing, is in the fabrication process, it is the link to the ateliers, the organic process of making clothes. As mentioned before, today it is not completely missing but its importance has considerably diminished. The artisanal process where you sculpted the clothes on the shape of the body has vanished to a great extent. In a way, they all start with the same elements, like in music where you have eight notes and with them you can make a symphony, elevator music or a punk song by using the exact same ones in different order or rhythm... and that's what fashion was in the eighties.

All these designers had their own obsessions, vocabulary and interpretations of the body. Saint Laurent was about elegance, sensuality, luxury in the noble sense of materials and skill, then Mugler who was very into futuristic show-girls, Moschino was into insolent caricatures, Montana was into his own designs and the girls had to act and pose exactly like his illustrations, etc. — but they all built with the same elements: the shoulder, the waist, the hips, the proportions of the body and they all preferred women with personality, with a bit or a lot of drama, exoticism, mystery, each expressing it with her runway style; there always was a narrative element to the image of "their" woman. They appreciated the silhouette that would suit their needs but they wanted an incarnation in their clothes, someone alive with a specific personality. Sometimes they would even find these qualities in someone who had less experience, a debutant, a street musician, an acrobat...

EMOTION

FM: Can you manoeuvre emotion through modelling or while posing for a photo shoot?

VS: Yes of course. It depends also on the emotions you think about. In my case, having been an actress before I was a model, I often carried that to the runway, even subliminally, embodying a character, based on the clothes they would put on, for the three minutes I was on the runway.

Certain designers asked for that specifically, Mugler, Moschino and Saint Laurent always said of me "Oh she is not a model, she is an actress" and they would always talk to me as that.

FM: How long does it take for a model to be 100 per cent conscious of what she/he is wearing?

VS: I would say that some of them never do, they don't have enough time or natural inclination to develop this relationship. Others don't care; they are not interested in that, they are more focused on themselves, being stars, you know... Also the fact of having to do five shows a day you can't get to truly become attached to what you are wearing.

When you are in the presence of strong, outstanding art, everybody in the room feels the same. The models that did very well on the runway, were those who were 100 per cent conscious of the clothes. If you gave me something fantastic to wear, believe me I would do a fantastic job. If you gave me something really mediocre, I would still do a very good job, the best I could, because that's what I was paid for but also for my reputation. Sometimes this would also be a sentimental obligation towards the designer, to help him or her out. There would be photographers at the end of the runway no matter what, and once you were hired you had to do your best, you actually put a very conscious effort into it.

Going back to emotion and photography, it's a very important connection, you are not producing the image by yourself, like you do on the runway, you have someone across the field that has to be inspired by you in order to produce something that is worth. The communication of that emotion is super relevant to the success of an image.

When we worked with film, pre-digital era, emotion was vital because it formed the alchemy in the team between the photographer, the model, the hairstylist, the make-up artist, the stylist, the assistant, all crucial parts of the result, some more than others, but none dispensable.

The expression after a successful shot was "We have it, you can change", which meant that the shot also contained the necessary level of emotions! The polaroid indicated whether we were ready to start shooting, if the inspiration was there and everything looked good, all the rest was built on emotion, trust, professionalism and talent. Then the first lights-test would arrive in the early afternoon and you could be sure that what you had done so far was technically sound.

Today the photographer often hardly looks at you; he is looking mostly at the screen, with constant interruptions of the energy flow to check it out, this constant necessity for immediateness. No magic, no suspense, no danger, what you see is what you get, which makes you feel that you are doing it in a sort of void, no depth, no mystery. Very little eye contact, paradoxically...

FM: I wonder if you were ever interested in observing how the audience perceives your work in fashion or in theatre?

VS: I am very emotional, so I am at my best when I do not communicate, I have to be very careful, because eye contact with the public distracts me, I lose my concentration and it breaks the spell, I always need to be in a spell, a little trance of my own if you want. Sometimes though, people talk to me and are extremely funny, it is exhilarating, inspiring in a theatrical way.

FM: Could we suggest clothing is a living organism?

VS: Clothes are much of a living organism the same as materials in the atelier of an artist are. Because of the different assemblage, the different uses you make of it, the iconoclast you can manifest. I have worked a lot with people who would disturb any order, who would divert any meaning and the first one was Moschino. I remember us at three in the morning shooting the campaign and taking the story in all directions, wearing the clothes upside down, making a jacket with a pair of trousers, my arms in the legs let's say, and this would give him ideas for his next season's collection. So yes, clothes are living organisms, they are creatures, little Frankensteins all of them. Since my adolescence, not having the financial means to purchase what was fashionable, I would buy and transform vintage/second hand, ensemble it, cut it, put it in the washing machine and shrink it because in the end it doesn't matter if nothing comes out of it, it is a creative iconoclastic process. If it doesn't work, it doesn't work.

I was very inspired by cinema or literature heroines, to this day I have my Virginia Woolf outfit, brogues, twin set and mid-calf tweed skirt, home-made in the eighties after a trip to Scotland.

POLITICS

FM: How would you describe the current state of fashion and why?

VS: I feel that for the moment it's on a survival mode. The lifeline is almost flat. They go from one season to the next like they're lost. The fashion world is totally dominated now by a few groups that make the rules, like an armada that has lost its compass. They use their designers as soccer players, who move from one team to the next. How can you move somebody from Balenciaga to Vuitton and then say "Let's see what happens"? I am not totally against it, its experimental interest is valid, but it shouldn't be systematic. Fashion today is genetically modified fashion, cloned on this or that DNA.

It doesn't make any sense anymore. Then you have the young designers who are idealistic, you go to the festivals, you see all those prizes but you can tell they are already geared towards getting noticed and getting integrated into the system. We hear a lot about team spirit, corporate, DNA.

If you turn all of that in a different way it actually equals to no individuality whatsoever, no human disturbance, it is all about control, product adjustments to the market. You are a corporation with a DNA, there is a team spirit but the individuals either disappear or can be brutally displaced or replaced in a very short time. This means that designers move — they used to be called stylists. Stylist is a new profession, that for the time being rules strongly; casting, styling of the outfits for the runway. Crucial aspects of the show that used to belong to the studio and the stylist/designer, and now are dispatched to someone who styles for various houses at the same time, turning shows into pages of a catalogue! I heard one say to a designer once "I need more trousers there!", which absolutely horrified me! Can you imagine YSL, Margiela, or a Galliano, Gaultier, Mugler being told such a thing? They are very powerful and also adjustable at the same time.

So what matters for all these people that move around like prawns, is the brand and furthermore the group it belongs to.

FM: What about the way fashion is formed today? Who is really directing it in your opinion?

VS: The industry, and it has lost all genuine eccentricity or element of surprise.

FM: Is there room for fantasy today? How can we keep that doorway open for it?

VS: Survival! Since you cannot exist if a large group does not sustain you, then that's it. The mass is over. In the seventies, the eighties you could develop yourself as a young designer because a magazine would give you a double spread, an editor would believe in you and that would help you start a small line and there would be a following for the seasons to come, you would build slowly the production, find financiers and the proportions remained human. The emotions remained human.

FM: Would you agree that fashion, now more than ever before, has become self-referential, much more secluded and closed and entirely for the fashionistas?

VS: Most definitely! It's what I was saying before about streetwear and how people don't make an effort to dress. Today designers link themselves with terms like family or army. There's this sense of planned obsolescence, there's a price to everything. If you buy a washing machine, it's not going to last for more than a year after the guarantee is over. It's the same for everything we buy, unless of course you make it yourself and you decide how long it will last.

Things are not meant to last, look at the perfumes or cosmetics in limited editions, they come out with every season, if you don't buy them now you will not be able to find them in three months and so on, so although you buy them you cannot appropriate them, make them yours, they cannot belong to your personality, you will not be recognisable through your scent, it will always be a different one. They've boosted this frenzy, this restlessness in people's minds, also the fact that what is more representative today of a fashion house is the accessories and bags. There is no reincarnation in a bag! A jacket, a coat, or a dress is very sensual. Your skin, your movement, your smell can be put in clothes. You cannot put anything in a bag other than your phone and home keys.

This total disincarnation that you see on the models when they walk like robots but also in the use of fashion we make.

The fashionistas are not normal people; they are soldiers of that fashion army these designers talk about. And we haven't mentioned H&M and Zara, that also have a huge impact on the distortion of fashion! Why would I be fascinated by a coat from Margiela, eventually buy it and keep it forever, when three months later there will be an acceptable and much cheaper version of it, in one of these fast-fashion shops? And I will see the adulterated, vulgarised, normalised version of it in the streets. Of course this rip-off, although it is now accessible, lacks the weight, the density, the make, the class of the original, but who cares? We need to learn looking at things and how they are done; we need to learn again to appreciate the craft, the work, the beauty for self-respect, if not anything else.

FM: How does wearing or demonstrating fashion help you/us understand society? What are the needs covered through fashion?

VS: Fashion in the first place, under the guise of individual taste, immediately conveys filiations or allegiance to a social group, chosen or born in it. It can be used as a disguise to pertain to a group but that usually only fools the non-members. Fashion is also a way to satisfy the need for society to classify and promptly recognise you.

In a world dominated by security concerns and simplistic psychology, what fashion you choose to follow is a basic ID.

Going back to what you mentioned earlier about fashion being "self-referential"... Indeed we now experience the fact of being dominated by the brand talking about the brand all the time, as opposed to before when the brand would try to make people attractive, and therefore gain their attention.

The Maisons de Mode had recognisable traits (Burberry check, Chanel initial, etc.), but the main object and purpose once was to satisfy certain canons of aesthetics of the moment in order to sell. For instance until the seventies a prominent bust was preferred, something society encouraged probably because it linked to maternity, butts were more discreet or on the contrary exaggerated and false towards the end of the nineteenth century, the "faux-cul" which is an insult in French, meaning hypocritical... but I'm digressing. It was all very much centred on the body and how to give it the desired and desirable shape required by the taste of the time, then it was about liberating it and in that sense that was the moment when fashion started to become a tool of empowerment for women to be themselves. Of course they had to comply with looking good, etc., but it was also geared to give them more freedom, like when YSL proposed for them "Le smoking" and men's suits, symbolically, being attractive without cleavage, legs or any visible flesh, was a step forward.

In some cases fashion was about expressing yourself and your rebellion, to make a social statement about who you were in the society, what were your ambitions, your opinions... In that way fashion was almost becoming political with the punk movement, the hippie movement and so on.

The most political we get today is through the gangsta and rapper songs of protest, which on the other hand are often super offensive to women, where those badass rebels also wear 10,000 dollars sneakers and very codified outfits, which in spite of their bagginess leave very little wiggle room for creativity. The girls wear sparse spandex, maybe a pair of Louboutin's, on very altered bodies — plastic surgery, tattoos and prosthesis have replaced fashion like there's no tomorrow...

FM: One of the designers that you worked closely with was of course Franco Moschino, whom you have already mentioned. He was a designer that would often pass his message out on T-shirts prints that he sent on the runway, like the British Katharine Hamnett, who was another rebel in that sense.

VS: You know, at some point he had a show where he was showing fur and he asked the models to walk out on all fours, and made a statement out of it! If you wear animal skin then you should walk like an animal! It's the least you can do.

Franco was a soft rebel and he liked to make fun of the fashion system, the fashion victims and the clothes while his approach would often be very kitsch and always benevolent. But he also loved fashion and women and elegance so I would dare to pair him with Margiela — not that their aesthetics have anything to do with one another, but they both started to divert the use of existing garments or the materials they are made with. For instance we had a shooting for a jeans collection and he created an entire Pope outfit made of denim, in Italy it was very iconoclastic.

He made statements, not so much against fashion as to put it back into perspective. Margiela's approach was also a do-it-yourself, recycle proposal, although his beautiful tailored coats were the best and could only be achieved by skilled professionals.

Moschino's recycling of certain styles and clothes, like creating jackets out of trousers, or making an evening gown out of garbage bags indicated to people "Ok, the stuff in my shop is very expensive but you can do it yourself too" and to the fashion world, "Don't take yourselves so seriously, it's all a joke."

Moschino came from the art world, he went to the Beaux-Arts before he moved to fashion and somehow he perhaps was challenging people's way of thinking and tried to make them more critical through his creations. Fashion is for everyone and it should be this way! Again, his work was a rebellion not against fashion but against the system. Adorning one's body using garments is a way of communicating with one another or to express something, it could be the mood of the day, it could be something you saw in the papers that made you dress that way because you felt you wanted to say something about it, this is how he saw things. He was fighting a system that today has totally gotten out of hand.

FM: So, having said that, what you think could cause a real revolution today? Everything today is a short-term project.

VS: I have been thinking about this a lot lately, with the recent fashion week! Not only me but also my friends who are on the decisive side of fashion, who work in fashion houses. They are puzzled and worried while one of their main concerns is where we are going and how can this evolve.

Also, the structure of the business now has become enormous, everybody is buying buildings and expanding.

The riding wave seems like the 2008 crash, the balance is off, somehow it's resting more and more on accessories, not so much on clothes — this is why for example the second-hand luxury market has developed on the internet. To buy the new "it" handbag every other season people need to sell their previous one because they can't otherwise afford it. This helps the market in one way as at the end of the day these people keep buying instead of keeping their expensive bag for years. It is also quite democratic because someone who could never afford that "it" bag when it's freshly released, six months or a year later will get it on the internet at a fraction of its original price. So, I don't know what to say, from the point of view of the clothes themselves, because what I see in the designs today is what we said before when we were talking about the body, its decreasing individuality, its total submission to market imperatives, creativity captive like a beautiful slave, chosen by the king, but a slave nevertheless.

I am feeling that the body is getting more and more secondary. One can say it used to be secondary when it was tortured by corsets or by whatever kind of clothing that would deform it or complied it. But at least the body was the earth you made the sculpture with. In the course of a workshop I recently did with students in a design school, the kids had been working on their mannequins and on themselves trying their stuff out, and the project was a bit stagnant.

When I showed up as a "professional body" it gave a new dynamic to the workshop that it didn't have before because I showed them the purpose of their clothes, the flaws, the strengths, etc. I made them alive.

Today you feel that this professionalism has disappeared in the sense that the in-house girls who fit the clothes, do it the same way the shows are done, as neutral as possible, no posing, no interpretation, they just stand there, so there seems to be no transition of any message between the designer, the garment, the body and the audience. There is very little or no connection at all.

The models today are not helping neither are they asked to help these clothes, if you see my point. Whenever by accident I find myself doing that, when trying something for someone that is not entirely finished, they are fascinated because my instinct tells me to inhabit the stuff and immediately appropriate it and test it somehow. I guess my history allows me, gives me the authority to do so, but it is what was expected of us young models in the eighties and nineties.

When I find myself backstage at a show, during hair and make-up most girls do not follow this fantastic process of their transformation as they are plugged in and when possible looking at their screens, totally submissive and hardly interested, as their social media requires their constant devotion, and their opinion or taste is not required, the atmosphere is obedient and unengaged. This is not their fault though; this is how they were groomed.

Also, the body is lost not only for the technical things but also because young designers today have a very short span to make themselves noticed by a large group, so they find ways that make them stand out. It's not so much about the body as it is about making a statement that will attract attention by the media.

If in that process they can make girls look good and feel good it's OK but I feel it's not their main purpose now. I say girls, because I am not so familiar with men's fashion.

If we compare them with how young designers worked twenty–thirty years ago, their goal was to embrace the woman or man they would design for. They would come out of fashion school with this ideal of their woman, they were very different from each other: some were romantic, others were futuristic, fairytalish, boyish, glamorous, whatever. They tried to make this woman they had in mind exist through their clothes. Of course they wanted also to be noticed and be financed. But back then it was also the time when things would still be discovered, invented, now everything seems to have been said!

I wonder how a new revolution would be and look like. Technological perhaps? Unisex?

Will these big groups allow a revolution or do we have to surpass them and make it ourselves?

VALERIE STEELE

Director and Chief Curator of The Museum at FIT,
Editor in Chief of Fashion Theory

BODY

FILEP MOTWARY: Dr. Steele, how would you say exhibiting fashion serves in understanding the body? What about our society?

VALERIE STEELE: I think that fashion is very much an embodied phenomenon. We really can only imagine fashion in relation to the body. Therefore, showing it in an exhibition is interesting because we disassociate it from the living body and instead we're showing it on other forms or mannequins; which are kind of puppets or dolls, inanimate forms on which we show clothes. That can be problematic and for many people fashion in museums seems dead.

To me however, it seems very useful as another way to get us to think about fashion and therefore also about the body/clothes unit.

Because instead of thinking of fashion as something that you are wearing or as something that you see your colleagues wearing, or something that you see on a screen, or as you are looking at Instagram or in a store, suddenly in the museum you are forced to observe clothes from the outside.

Whenever possible, we can make it that you are able to walk around the garment on a mannequin or a dress, other times we place mirrors — so you can see it from different angles, to think about it perhaps more abstractly.

Last Fall (2017–18), my colleague Emma McClendon curated the exhibition "The Body: Fashion and Physique" which called attention specifically to the relationship between fashion and the body and how fashion has preferred at different times different types of bodies and created as it were facsimiles of the ideal body whether through pattern, padding, etc.

McClendon explored how that was done through corseting, through padding-out the clothes with things like bustles. More recently, diet and exercise modify the body. Now there is a new movement to try to see whether the fashion industry can be more accommodating to a range of different body types, the so-called "plus-size fashion" (as many women in the world are larger than standard fashion sizes) and how fashion is coming to terms with that. She chose to put everything on dress forms and not on mannequins. We could have gone for plus-size mannequins, but it's more abstract on dress forms, which can be expanded or shrunken, thus showing how clothing fits on different bodies.

FM: How did the contemporary silhouette, as we know it, get defined?

VS: Until the twentieth century there was much greater gender distinction between male and female silhouettes. Men's legs were featured in fashion and women's legs were concealed under a skirt. So the skirt became a kind of base structure on top of which you had a stylised version of the sexually-dimorphic female torso — so an exaggeration of the female waist-hip differential, what we call an hourglass figure.

In the early twentieth century, the hourglass shifted to a more straight up-and-down silhouette. Sometimes fashion emphasises on sexual dimorphism more and sometimes it tilts towards androgyny, emphasising the things that male and female bodies have in common: two arms, two legs, etc.; often certain features are stressed, such as a man's broad shoulders or a woman's relatively narrow waist in comparison with wider hips.

FM: Somehow fashion was much more elaborate, historically speaking, when it came to menswear and then it was women that fashion put its focus on...

VS: It's really fascinating because if you look at it in world-historical terms, throughout most of history, men's fashion was at least as elaborate and stylish as womenswear, if not more so. Usually more so, because men had the power and the money, and women were constrained, by issues of modesty and, of course, the fact that they usually didn't have an independent source of income.

The shift toward more sober male attire begins in the middle of the eighteenth century and then takes over by the middle of the nineteenth century. It's complicated but to give a very simple answer, it's the result of capitalism and democracy. Hitherto, it was the split between the aristocracy and the masses that mattered and male and female aristocrats were equally decorative, or the men slightly more decorative.

Afterwards, with more democratic and bourgeois society, men became brothers ruling jointly instead of serving the "king father". Women were kept out of politics and became purely decorative.

Decoration was no longer a sign of power. Women were now being decorative on behalf of the men who were now serious moneymaking and politically engaged brothers. There's a shift from class or status to gender and because of that, women then served as the repository of all the colour, the decoration, the jewellery that were previously associated with a man's privilege.

FM: Throughout history humans have been praising the human body as nature's masterpiece and also suggesting a few improvements for various reasons and challenges. Why do body standards change over the years while certain attributes remain as classics? What forces these changes in your opinion? (From "The Birth of Venus", c. 1486, by Botticelli, to Marie Antoinette, Louise Brooks, Bettie Page, Twiggy, Kim Kardashian...)

VS: There are differences and there are similarities. Take Marilyn Monroe, Twiggy and the contemporary fashion model Elle McPherson:

although their weight and the size of their breasts and bottoms are very different, their waist-hip differential are virtually identical point-seven. The preference for a clearly feminine waist-hip differential may be hardwired into human beings for obvious evolutionary reasons. If our ancestors had made it with pre-pubescent females or pregnant females or post-menopausal females, we wouldn't be here, because the genes would have run out. There was a very important need to mate with sexually fertile, nubile, young women. So, the waist-hip differential is very important.

Other aspects such as breast or bottom size have varied depending on what was regarded as beautiful in any given place and time. This would depend in large part on sexual selection, so if you had a group which was sexually selective for larger bottoms, that body type would start to emerge. In many cases in European history, we see clear evidence of how clothing styles influenced the body ideal.

This is because historically we have gotten an idea of what the ideal body should look like, not by looking at a lot of naked bodies, but rather by looking at clothed bodies. We see how the shape of the nude in historical images corresponds with the shape of the clothing. Anne Hollander was the first to realise that we were seeing clothed people and then drawing from that the idea of what the nude should be like. Even as late as the seventies, all those long slim legs in tight blue jeans influenced the nudes created by artists like Philip Pearlstein.

Sometimes you will see there is a moment when young people are more active and trendsetting, such as in the twenties and the sixties, where the ideal clearly becomes a younger thinner body.

In the nineteenth century when really only married women had the wherewithal and the permission to dress fashionably, the ideal was voluptuous Venus. In the early twentieth century, the ideal shifted to an athletic, young Diana figure. Some of the same things happened with men. Older people in Italy still use the expression "you look prosperous" to praise a leaner body whereas younger people think you are supposed to be athletic, you are rich enough to be athletic. In the past, the people who did hard physical labour work weren't so much made strong as they were made exhausted, and broken down by labour. Of course if you are golfing and sailing and playing tennis or cycling, then you are creating a new kind of more mesomorphic body that can be idealised.

FM: What about the technological body, the body that is dressed by computerised clothing? Why does the human still need to look and act human?

VS: There are a couple of ways to approach that, because the technological body has long been both a fear and an ideal for humans. In the early twentieth century, we saw that with mechanisation taking control not only of industry but of the idea, human movement was more mechanised. For example, Busby Berkeley displays were machine-like in unison.

But the technological body also can be an ideal, because machines lack vulnerability, lack blood and flesh that can be wounded and die. So there is the idea that a hard body, some kind of prosthetic robot-like body, might be better.

I think we see, especially with women whose bodies have been subject to more social control, an internalisation of corsetry in the twentieth and twenty-first centuries. Instead of having a hard whalebone armature or a metal corset just pushing the fat around, we internalise the idea of a hard body through diet and exercise and later plastic surgery. You can have a six-pack carved through plastic surgery on your torso to make it look as though you have rippling muscles.

FM: How in your opinion did Diana Vreeland infuse athleticism into fashion magazines in such a remarkable way that we still use her examples as ideals today?

VS: As early as the thirties, in fashion photographs, we see women running instead of posing quietly, and I think that this idea of the body's coiled energy about to move is very powerful. Images of models running give a sense of power. In fact, fashion designers sometimes prefer to show their clothes on dancers or athletes, because athletes are in some ways our ideal of what the body is supposed to be like.

FM: How connected are fashion designers today to the body they design for?

VS: I think most designers have a very clear sense about the body for which they are designing. They choose a particular fitting model on which to create their clothes; that is the first clue. Then it's the model they choose to present these clothes on the runway. Models are increasingly supposed to be clothes-hangers and not so much personalities like the supermodels of the past. Lastly, there are the models for advertisements. So those are three ways that you envision the ideal of the individual designer. Many designers have had, I think, very restricted and restrictive ideals, very young and very thin models.

Even when they make larger sizes, there's usually a limit on how large they are willing to go. I remember hearing about one famous designer who when a model came in — and I am sure that compared to most women she was still slim and tall and model-like — rejected her by saying "I don't dress furniture".

FM: How relevant is the principle of covering the female body to conceal it from the male gaze today?

VS: Historically, the female body has been subject to a patriarchal control, including the idea that enforced modesty and the concealment of the female body are socially required both to maintain female chastity and to control male lust.

In other words to keep society under control. In some cultures this belief is still very strong, while in other cultures considerable body exposure is normative. However, each culture draws limits, it's not necessarily because of body shame but because of ideas of what is appropriate in different contexts. So, for example in the seventies, you saw people wearing hot pants even in the office. Nowadays I think few HR departments would permit that. Few people would find it appropriate to wear a bikini at the office. It would be appropriate to wear it on the beach — at least in some cultures. For example in Brazil you see the little "dental-floss" bikinis that are so skimpy on the bottom but if you went topless in Brazil you would be arrested. Meanwhile in France women literally go topless on the beach but the skimpy bottom is regarded as quite shocking. So this is very much contextual, as each society negotiates which parts of the body to cover.

Nowadays you also have the feminist movement asking whether the exposure of the body is liberating for women or whether it is a kind of self-objectification. An art gallery owner said that if she is wearing a mini skirt, then a wealthy collector might hit on her, so she tries to wear clothes which are relatively body concealing that will emphasise that she's an intellect and he is buying her expertise and not buying her body.

FM: Can the clothes be more advanced than the body that wears them?

VS: It's not so much a question of the body but the person that wears them. Certainly somebody who is in their thinking not particularly progressive or avant-garde, could make a decision to buy clothes that make them appear like a more progressive or avant-garde person. I remember being shocked that Comme des Garçons sold very well in Texas. It didn't fit my idea of what Texas women looked like.

EMOTION

FM: How can we manoeuvre emotion through fashion? Where in your opinion does fashion meet with emotion? Does imagination currently fit in the context of fashion?

VS: Emotion interacts with fashion in many ways. For example, when you put on a certain garment and feel good about yourself, you feel confident. I remember the Spanish designer Sybilla saying to me once that "If you put on a red dress on a grey morning, it transforms your mood. Suddenly instead of being blocked you feel you could go out and eat the world", meaning that you are full of energy and confidence. There is also the display of emotion in the presentation of fashion. Runway shows used to be more theatrical; we all remember John Galliano and Alexander McQueen and earlier Thierry Mugler's shows. Today only a few companies like Chanel and Dior can still afford elaborate shows. It is not the same though now, as there is more emphasis on the brand rather than the theatrical fantasy per se. Formerly, there was the "go for broke" madness about it and you could be very extreme and risk, angering and upsetting people.

People got quite upset by a lot of those shows: "How dare McQueen or Galliano do a show like that, it's shocking, it's immoral, it's unacceptable". Reactions as such were very common.

Now people don't want to risk that kind of backlash. For most designers, it is expensive enough to do the most banal girls-walk-out-girls-walk-back show. There are also many more shows today; with 200 shows in a week you can no longer have a show that is big and long and elaborate. Shows used to be much longer!

FM: Do you think this is going to change?

VS: Well, I don't see any clear way that, say, New York Fashion Week can cut back on the number of shows. The French do it because they are very top-down. But in the US, if you can afford to put on a show, then you can do it. It seems more democratic to allow everyone to do their own shows, but there are more and more companies, manufactures, as well as creative designers that are putting on shows now unlike the past. There are just too many shows. Another way of presenting fashion will have to emerge; but so far, fashion films have not really given the sense of excitement of a live fashion show.

FM: What about this democratic turn that fashion took?

VS: It is the direction the world is going. You have all the bloggers, many more voices in fashion now. With fast fashion, you have the accessibility of the current fashion, being immediately out there for millions of people. Perhaps, there will eventually be a turn towards slow fashion. If we have more and more fashion shows, maybe it is time to have fewer and better fashion shows. Maybe designers should act the way musicians do. Musicians only put out a new record when they are ready to. It could be once a year, once every two years. There is no question that creative people need to recharge. The endless cycle of fashion shows does not give designers time to recharge and think through precisely what they want to do for the next collection. Some of them have barely a week to rest after a show and they immediately start designing the next one!

FM: Why is the ceremonial process of dressing linked with achieving a higher state of feelings?

VS: I think that there is a sense that dressing is a way of presenting your humanity, your individuality. It is the creation of the public persona that you are presenting to the world. Some people object to that and say that clothing ought to be more "natural", that it ought to be a reflection of your "true" inner self. But, how can you say there's inner self apart from your interactions with others? Clothing lies on the border between your inner subjectivity and that of other people around you, so it's always going to be a way of trying to present yourself to them. It's a form of indirect communication! More like music rather than language, it creates opportunities for a particular mood or feeling.

FM: Could we suggest clothing is a living organism and in what ways?

VS: You know, there's a wonderful science fiction book from the seventies by Barrington J. Bayley titled "The Garments of Caean", obviously playing on the idea of the Biblical Cain, about clothes which come alive and, like the computer in Kubrick's "2001: A Space Odyssey", get up to no good. Clothes are like an expression of us: how we're feeling, how we're thinking, who we think we are, they don't have any agency in themselves.

When people write "Oh, fashion does bad things to us", they refer to it like it's some kind of monster taking over us. There's no monster as such doing stuff to you. We are the ones who are creating fashion and deciding what fashions are successful. The designers propose it but really it's everybody else who decides whether they want sneaker X or sneaker Y or a high-heel shoe, people are the ones who choose and always have.

FM: How is desire integrated into fashion?

VS: It can be a question of clothing that is supposed to inspire desire in other viewers. Remember Galliano's famous line about how he wanted to make clothing that would make people really think, "Oh, I really wanna fuck her!" It could as well be a question of desire to buy those clothes which is certainly the kind of desire that most designers and companies want to inspire. Because we don't need more clothes, we just have the desire to buy something new. It could be something else about the clothes that we don't just desire to buy them — which could be a temporary, sometimes very temporary gratification — but a feeling of happiness and joy wearing those clothes over a period of time. It makes you desire to pull out your favourite shirt out of the closet and wear it over and over. You've got 99 other shirts but you think "today is an important day so I'd really rather wear that shirt".

FM: At which point in fashion we feel most vulnerable?

VS: Wearing a bathing suit, I should say, for most people. I mean if you think of shoe shopping as the ultimate form of pleasurable shopping, you are never too old or too fat to buy a beautiful pair of shoes, some people don't even care if they can walk in them, really. When I talk to people about buying shoes, they just want the shoes.

But, if you buy something like a bathing suit, it brings out people's insecurities about their bodies. There are also many people, men especially but also women who just feel a kind of a panic attack when they enter into the store thinking, "What the hell am I going to buy?".

Shopping online has become very popular for many people as a way of avoiding that horrible anxiety of going into the store and feeling overwhelmed by all of choices: "Can you afford this, can you fit in that, are you being an idiot, will you regret this", all these kinds of fears people have when they are shopping. Online shopping avoids a lot of that. In your home, it's less painful, you are not facing the sales person who might be trying to talk you into buying something so she could get a commission.

With online shopping, you just put it in the box and send it back, if it doesn't work. For many it's a relatively pain-free way of shopping.

FM: How can we overcome ourselves through dressing while avoiding obsolescence?

VS: There is a certain tension between the idea of I. following fashion and renewing yourself with each new fashion and 2. developing your own style. Many ordinary people, as they get older, create a personal style. There is, however, the danger for example of never changing your hairstyle or looking frozen in time. I think everybody makes a different decision about that. It may be that you decide there are certain types of garments, certain designers whom you like but you are willing to move along with them. You know, if you like trench coats you buy one every few years but it won't be the identical one.

Young people tend to be neophiliacs, they love what is new. The Japanese are wonderful that way; they want the newest thing constantly. Young people like the new new new, but they also tend to buy cheap cheap cheap, so the clothes are disposable. They can get something new every week.

FM: The ways models present fashions on the catwalk changes every decade. It seems that in the past we had ceremonial moments, at times very lively, dance was even incorporated on the runway etc.

VS: In the early days of the Couture, it was very ceremonial, very stylised, look number one would be read out and the model would hold her number.

Even then, there was sometimes drama: I remember reading about a Dior show "the skirt might sweep the ashtrays off the journalists tables" back in the forties and fifties when they were smoking at the shows. With the youth revolution in the sixties and early seventies, the shows were much more music-oriented and much more about physicality through a more diverse range of models. You had the superstar models in the late eighties and early nineties. Now most designers want the girls to fall into the background, so that our attention is focused on the clothes and not on the personality of the model.

Donatella recently offered a homage to the Versace past by bringing back some of the supermodels. The audience loved that, because it was a blast from the past. It worked for that show, but it wouldn't have if it were replicated in other shows. I think we are starting to see some designers add a greater diversity of models on the catwalk in terms of race, body size, and age. This in turn may lead to a greater diversity of self-presentation on the runways. It will need to be something that works itself out organically according to the vision of the designer and the stylist as they work on each individual show. Only a few designers really focus on the show. Thom Browne, for example, said that he wouldn't do fashion if he couldn't do the fashion show. Most designers design the collection and then they put the show together. McQueen thought of the show first and then the collection!

POLITICS

FM: How is fashion revelatory of the social mechanism and politics?

VS: Fashion is a part of our time, but that doesn't mean that every political shift or every socio-economic event will be apparent in fashion. Historical events are one set of causes that influence fashion, art, and literature. There are also influential individuals, that are brilliant designers, brilliant singers who capture the public's attention. But the third cause of change is the most important one: we have the professional world where designers look at what other designers do, they look at what other designers have success with. Then they also look at what their clients are doing and what their clients are dressing for, if the clients are skateboarding, if the clients are going out clubbing, if they are staying home to socialise. These are the biggest influences on fashion.

If politics become so intrusive that it affects how you live, if you go out on the street wearing something, which is for some reasons forbidden, you will be physically attacked and have the clothes ripped off from your body, as happened in China during the Cultural Revolution — that will certainly influence the clothes that you wear! You are not going to go out twice and be attacked like that! I was attacked on the street in New York once by an anti-fur person; he came up and grabbed me and shook me and I was terrified. I ended up giving the fur coat to my mother because she lived in another state where people would give her a thumbs up and say "Nice fur!" Unless politics impinges directly on you, it is really more what are you doing in your life that influences your style.

FM: What about the way fashion is formed today? Who is directing it?

VS: Fashion is no longer a top-down phenomenon, if it ever was, and even back at Dior's day he said, "The designer proposes but the ladies dispose", the ladies decide what's successful. Today most designers are desperately trying to figure out what people want to buy. Retailers also don't want to have to put everything on sale; they want to figure it out. The customer is not sure either, what he or she wants, how much he or she wants to pay. Everybody is a little bit unsure now.

FM: Why do you think this happens?

VS: We have too much. It's a very clear psychological thing. Psychology has shown that people love choice, they don't want to be in a country where you have only one shampoo you can buy, they want a choice of shampoo, a choice of clothes; but if the choice gets too big, if you are facing 200 hundred choices of shampoo, 200 kinds of yogurts or sweaters, then you flip and go "What the fuck, I don't need another yogurt, another sweater." When you have to buy a shampoo you close your eyes and say, "I'm going to buy this one." Too much choice is confusing and disturbing to people, that's why some stores are able to keep a customer base because they say "Don't worry, I will select from amongst these 200 things and bring you down to 15 very cool designers and looks and you can choose amongst that." Certain stores like Dover Street Market get very loyal customers.

FM: Would you agree that fashion has become self-referential?

VS: Not really, because it's also become much more open. We have on the one hand fashion people talking to each other and on the other hand you have the refusal of the masses of people to just follow dictates from editors and designers.

FM: Think of someone like YSL or Gianni Versace, their work was so powerful, so well communicated that even my grandmother knew who they were. It was something for her to wear their perfume or to own a shawl for example. Today's designers are not welcomed to everybody's house as something special like it used to be, even as a notion.

VS: Yes, that is very true and it's because the "empire of fashion" has broken up into multiple style tribes. That was already happening in the seventies. I wore Comme des Garçons or Yohji Yamamoto or Norma Kamali in the early eighties and people would go "What is that, what are you wearing?" It was meaningless to them, as they never heard of these designers. But it was a kind of secret Masonic handshake to others. There was a cult of avant-garde Japanese designers that "we" would know what we were doing! We'd go "Oh, what a cool Norma Kamali sweatshirt suit", something that was completely meaningless to others, who wondered "Why is your suit made of sweatshirt material?" Today most people only understand a few dialects in fashion. The 0.1%, the very rich people, understand Chanel, Louis Vuitton, and Hermès... They are oblivious to most of what happens in fashion or if they know Givenchy, for example, they do not know that Clare Waight Keller has replaced Riccardo Tisci. These are specific in-group fashion things that only fashion people know.

FM: Not more than twenty years ago, designers such as McQueen and John Galliano were creating entire collections inspired by tribes, global historical references, and folklore. Today this approach is considered as inappropriate. What happened in between?

VS: I think that people are becoming more conscious that cultural appropriation is problematic. In terms of fashion, there have been so many insulting rip-offs. When I was a child it was perfectly OK to run around playing Indians with a feather head-dress but over time, more and more Native Americans said "You know, it's our culture and you cannot just take it."

We see people in Mexico whose particular designs are just ripped off by a big company, without any attempt to monetise this for the group who actually created the design. So, I think that although extreme political correctness is problematic, there's also been so much unconscious racism and expropriation of other people's ideas that it was inevitable that there would be a backlash against that.

There is an idea that there should be a sense of responsibility on the part of the artists and designers to try to find more about their sources of inspiration, to communicate more with the people, who although they do not legally own the rights to something, nevertheless have some kind of moral or intellectual rights to say what ought to be done with it.

There's been such a racist discourse about black peoples' hair, for example, that it's not surprising many African Americans are highly conscious of the politics of hair. I think white people should try to understand what is going on there.

Some groups of people have been horribly oppressed and the people who oppressed them ought to think a little bit before they treat them like a Halloween costume!

FM: Today, we experience the phenomenon of the "designer tribe": Balmain, Rick Owens, Yohji Yamamoto, Comme des Garçons, Ann Demeulemeester, Dries Van Noten...?
How does this uniformity affect the society and how different designer uniformity is from working or school uniforms?

VS: The fact that we have people who are entirely devoted to the designs of a particular creator indicates a choice to say, "I am really involved in this kind of aesthetic, and I am this kind of person" and it involves an implied sense of values and ideals. "I like this kind of person because he/she is experimental, an independent designer and not part of a corporation."

Whatever the meaning is, you are associated with it and I think that it's not dissimilar to being associated with a particular music, or type of movie. You go like "I would never go to that movie" and people go "Why" and you say "It's just not me". So in a sense these clothes, these movies, this music, this kind of food, even the choice of friends identifies you. It's the notion of belonging, the notion of taste. If you think of it that way the food's taste it's part of your habitus but it's also how cosmopolitan you are, if you have learnt how to expand your taste to go beyond of what is considered the norm.

FM: In your opinion does the longevity of these "tribes" depend on the creative timeline of the designer's relevancy or will it be infinite?

VS: I don't think it's infinite, but it can certainly exceed the relevance of the style, just because people are not that quick to move on to a new style. Once they are used to seeing themselves in a certain look it takes something strong to move you away from that to say "No, I am not that kind of person anymore". When you have a new designer taking over a company and you might think "Oh well, not the same!", some people on the other hand would say, "That House used to be so boring", like last years of Chanel's life, it was very bourgeois style. After she died, it was still not as interesting, until the moment Lagerfeld stepped in and made Chanel exciting again.

The creative relevance of the house is important yet it's not the only feature to explain why people might continue to wear something.

FM: On the morning that followed the opening night of the Comme des Garçons show at the MET, Linda Evangelista posted a screenshot from what seemed like an sms conversation between two people talking about the event. The first asks how was Monday night and the latter says "Rei walked through the lobby on her way to the MET and NO ONE recognised her... they were all too busy by taking selfies and getting in line to get paparazzied outside the hotel..."
I wonder if at the end, knowing who is who in fashion is important or not?

VS: Important to whom and for what end? Obviously some players in the fashion world, including Andrew Bolton who chose to do a show on Comme des Garçons, recognised Rei Kawakubo. Clearly Rei wasn't on the radar for a lot of the MET Gala guests.

Nevertheless, many key players in the fashion world felt that Rei was one of, if not the most, creative figure in fashion today and deserved to be the first living designer in almost forty-five years to be given an exhibition at the Costume Institute. The last time this happened was in the eighties with YSL. It was a great coup actually for Andrew to say "She may not be famous to everybody but to key fashion people she is super important and deserves her own show". So whether other people knew about her or not, it didn't really matter, they didn't know about her anyway when she first became famous in the eighties when she was some sort of secret, and everybody asked "What's that black thing you are wearing?"

When the Japanese arrived in Paris in the eighties, people were hysterical. They were screaming that their clothes were an insult, that women should be beautiful and show off their gym-toned bodies. Hearing that somebody was covering it up with these "ugly" funereal rags, there was a lot or racist discourse about "Hiroshima Fashion". It was absolutely a shock, a real shock to the fashion system and yet now we go back and say "Wow, that was such an important fashion revolution" and ended up not only consolidating the influence of these Japanese avant-garde designers, but influencing everybody. Lagerfeld at Chanel couture does frayed edges, all of those things were taken initially from the Japanese, it's become part of fashion!

JUN TAKAHASHI_UNDERCOVER

Fashion designer, founder Undercover

BODY

FILEP MOTWARY: How can the body be trained in order to serve fashion?

JUN TAKAHASHI_UNDERCOVER: I run three times a week to keep my body in shape. This training is based on my idea that the basic silhouette is my body, especially for designing men's clothes.

FM: Allow me to go back in time and focus on your 2006 Autumn Winter collection where you presented a series of silhouettes that had their faces covered in bejewelled headdresses, which evoked historical references. The body somehow appeared as a glorified mummy while each look worked individually redefining the silhouette by its outlines and textures. Could you walk us back to that show, the inspiration at the time and how do you see this collection today?

JT: In the 2006 AW Guru Guru collection, part of the clothing was made extremely long to wrap around the body, which was the theme. The models were swathed in cloth, which is described as "Guru Guru" in Japanese. That show was very weird and eerie, so I like it very much.

FM: What about your tendency to present fashion on identical bodies, in sets of two, either on twins or models that look almost identical? How would you explain it?

JT: For the Languid collection (2004 Spring Summer) where I used twins, I showed usual clothing on one model and on the other the same design but extremely stretched out. As you see, I intended to show contrast. For the Janus collection (2018 Spring Summer), I dressed twins in reversible clothes — the front side on one twin and the reverse side on the other — again to show contrast. My idea is that the contrast becomes clearer on a twin with the same face and body shape.

FM: How is the meaning of the "body" approached in fashion, considering its permanent outline and the fact that it is something generic?

JT: The body could be just a figure for clothing. The human body takes a complicated shape, but if I view it from the point of enveloping it and also making designs that bring out its beauty, I feel a person's body is very mysterious.

FM: Is the corset a sign of authority onto the body? (2013 Autumn Winter Undercover)

JT: I didn't intend that. I just wanted to use it as a sexual element.

FM: How can we reform or re-apply the form of the modern body?

JT: I think the body is universal and there is no need to change it.

FM: Do we seek for a deeper meaning into clothing? Can fashion be didactic, and at what level?

JT: Since ancient times, people have thought about how to change their looks by using clothing. The messages clothing sends have changed from age to age. I think this is just repeated.

FM: What about the technological body, the body that is dressed by computerised clothing? Why does the body still need to look and act human?

JT: I am not interested in an excessively technologised body with a microchip embedded in it, but I am very interested in computerised clothing. I want to try designing clothes that use technology. For example, I quite agree with using high technology for disabled people. But I think an AI robot that looks exactly like a human is not necessary at all.

FM: We have been desperately exploring or trying to re-define the silhouette for centuries now. Humans have been working on reconstructing the body and proportion through clothing... Why this particular need?

JT: I think it is just for the pursuit of "beauty" in each era.

EMOTION

FM: How relevant is the principle of covering the female body to conceal it from the male gaze today?

JT: The view may be different from person to person, but I think it also includes an implication of a complex about body shape or the need for protection against unwanted sexual advances from men.

FM: What is so important about being new? Does creation have to be new?

JT: I don't think at all that everything should be new. But as far as I am concerned, I always keep in mind to "make a design that is new to me" in the sense that I create what I have never created before. It doesn't matter whether or not my design is new to the world.

FM: How did you manage to manoeuvre emotion through your 2017 Autumn Winter collection?

JT: In 2017 AW collection, I expressed a world where people live equally even though there are hierarchical classifications. Whether someone may be the king, a soldier, or a delinquent girl, they can co-exist in a spiritual sense without stress. If my intention got across, it can be said that I was able to manoeuvre the audience's emotion.

FM: What determines if something is surprising or emotional enough on the catwalk?

JT: I think it depends solely on the creator's will. I think that there is no excitement in a show which is just commercial or where only designs can be recognised. I always wish to shake up people's minds. This is my will as a creator.

FM: Where in your opinion fashion meets with emotion? What are the guiding principles?

JT: I think when a creator and those who pick up his or her clothing find a common element, their emotions are stirred.

FM: How can we overcome ourselves through dressing while avoiding obsolescence?

JT: You can overcome if you know your limitations, or yourself.

FM: Are you interested to hear how others observe what you create? How bonded are you with what you serve in fashion?

JT: I am very concerned about others' opinions. I think that what I have brought to the fashion world and what I want to communicate are relatively well bonded.

POLITICS

FM: How is fashion revelatory of the social mechanism and politics?

JT: I think it depends on whether or not creators want to express themselves in that way. I don't think all creators have to express their political will through their clothes.

FM: What about the way it is formed today? Who is directing it?

JT: Some designers project their political will in their designs, but I rarely bring my will to the fore.

FM: The word "intellectual" was coined at a time of extreme political anxiety. I wonder whether today, more than ever before, fashion has a political role? And in which way?

JT: The fashion genre is more tightly segmented than before. I think it is why some genres have more political features and may stand out.

FM: Is there any sort of hierarchy in fashion as you see it? Who is directing it?

JT: I feel hierarchy in the fashion business. Small companies like us and large companies are significantly different in terms of sales and PR exposure. But I want to see to what extent I will be able to leave my footsteps in the fashion world where the hierarchy exists.

FM: Should all fashion shows be enjoyable and optimistic?

JT: Even a dark, negative show arouses emotion in you. You may see it if you look at my show. I don't think at all that every show should be positive.

FM: How does fashion serve liberty and vice versa?

JT: Fashion serves liberty in that designers break rules in the process of creation. On the other hand, excessive design will eventually not be regarded as fashion.

FM: To what level we are conscious of what we see, buy, or wear? Does it matter?

JT: Answers may vary widely. Some people do not care about it at all. But I take it as being very important because I am a designer.

FM: We witness how the modern fashion model's posture has changed, the use of hands, and the choreography for the most part, is now a rather straight walking line. How would you explain this phenomenon and the reasons behind these changes, if we compare it to twenty, thirty, forty years back?

JT: Today, the show itself places great importance on commercial implications. I feel excessive posing is in the opposite direction from the sense of reality (on the premise of selling a sense of reality). I think it is a factor that has made straight walking the mainstream. This tells how important it is for business to be conscious of general people.

When emphasising business, "a sense of reality" is an essential element, isn't it? This trend can apply not only to walking, but also to hair, makeup, and staging. The meaning of shows probably has changed so much from the past. But I think my stance may be different from such shows.

FM: Models are always briefed before a show on how they should walk, how to use their hands, their head, what to avoid or where to emphasise. Why do shows need to be so dictatorial?

JT: Rather than dictatorial, I think it is natural for creators to ask models to do what and how in detail when they think of the show they want to create through using models.

FM: Would you agree that fashion, now more than ever before, has become self-referential, much more secluded and closed and entirely for those following fashion religiously?

JT: Unique brands have a religious element, regardless of the era. It is also a fact that, as I mentioned in "Q8", there is an overwhelmingly large number of commercial brands. A lot of companies, especially fast fashion, have become more and more open to people, so it is not necessarily appropriate to say that fashion has become more secluded.

OLIVIER THEYSKENS

Fashion Designer

BODY

FILEP MOTWARY: In your early steps, specifically in your OT 1998 Autumn Winter collection, you sent out three of your models wearing clothes that resembled the body from the inside. The body was viewed as if it was transparent, with its veins, the blood, and the heart; perhaps it was also a metaphor that resembled the roots of a tree. Could you kindly walk us back twenty years and share the process of this collection, from the perspective of the man you are today?

OLIVIER THEYSKENS: I remember very well when I did the first drawing of that outfit as it was made prior to the rest of that collection's ideas.

It was in Paris, I was at a friend's and I just drew this body with visible circular system. I was very excited, at first just by the idea of it. When I started drawing the whole collection I remember how I integrated the concept within the rest of the clothes from that show, as a natural process. When the idea was conceived in my mind, I wanted it to be embroidered, with just a thread that would start thin and would get thicker and thicker just like the veins, until it would reach the heart where I wanted this thread to create a lace motif.

In my mind, the lace motif represented the emotions of the heart. I conceptualised the idea by putting some emotional aspects inside and being an entirely dyslexic person I actually put the heart on the wrong side of the garment. There is no natural way to see it, I think it was how it was and I liked the look of it or how the girls wearing it would have this sort of heart, lace, veins and blood visible. At the time I was very much into anatomy books too and I think through this collection it was also a way to energise it as it was mostly about strong leather, extremely heavy and long dresses.

The "heart" outfit and a fur outfit gave certain energy to the rest; there was also a model that walked out in a fur look that had a bit of red details on it and it appeared as if she was bleeding.

There definitely was a certain attitude within this collection that was saying more than just "this is the trend and what women will be wearing for the next season".

This was anyway my first show in Paris and I wanted to present myself with a collection that was naturally strong and I was entirely disconnected from any sort of trend seeking, I just wanted to create and show that.

It was also about the use of materials for furniture or curtains, a lot of linen and bed sheets from my French Normandy family. I put all of what I had and it wasn't a collection where I chose fabrics from mills or went to a fabric fair to buy them. It was very personal actually.

FM: In OT spring 1999, one of your models wore a catsuit that resembled a naked body while the rest of the clothes reflected a very strong reference to fetishism. Are these subjects still interesting you today, and in what ways?

OT: Yes, the one you used in the exhibition you curated at the Modemuseum in Hasselt [Haute-à-Porter, 2016, curated by Filep Motwary]! I mostly have mixed feelings from that collection to be honest, as I was still in search of the direction I wanted to go creatively. In my mind it is filled with highlights and lowlights, especially when I think of the creative process. I came up with a million drawings but there were only a couple that I really felt strongly for. I was not in the mood to repeat myself and indeed there was some sort of continuity from where I started but at the same time I wanted to find a good and new point about this collection.

I remember that it was not an easy one to do and I wasn't so happy with it. The collection might appear sexual or fetishist but to be honest it was not conscious and I didn't even think to dig into that current or to find artists, image-makers and stories from that context to get inspired by. I was just drawing and I remember getting a little bit stuck with that, willing that they would look strong and comfort me in my vision. It was hard to start a creative dialogue between drawings and reality, I couldn't find exactly how to pick and continue it, how to make it fully finished. Even on the day of the show I didn't feel I had very much control on it and that reflects the state I was in, my self-transformation and exploration of being a young designer who just started to learn how to be commercial, myself dealing with factories in Italy while trying to make strong garments. I was dealing with a lot of things at the same time and not feeling very much secure about the collection, or me, as I remember. Certainly I was a happy boy and things were moving forward and I was full of energy, all memories are positive but I recall the creative and execution side and it was difficult then.

FM: What about today, when you look back at it, do you still have the same feelings? It was the collection that established you somehow, wasn't it?

OT: I still have the archives of the collection so when I look at it, there are outfits that I still like, there are drawings that I still like but there are also mistakes that today I consider as revelatory of how it goes when you don't have enough time to do fittings and how something that is not properly sewn in a factory looks like... Of course there are great pieces in this collection as well, some of my old time favourites are also there. The feelings are mixed.

It was an enterprise, even for producing it later it was a very rock'n'roll and bumpy road as I was an independent designer, there was a trillion solutions I had to come up with every day, it was tricky. It was also a very warm moment, as I had enormous support from my friends and I was working my ass off and skipping one or two nights a week. Those were really wild times. Parts of it were interesting, others even more, and for example I loved the hair of the girls at the show. It was kind of very like natural, which wasn't so common at the time as things were quite excessive in fashion. It might appear a stupid detail but that was the time when everybody had to be a little over-creative with everything, it was really new to have models with their hair a bit undone, that make up... They look timeless today's girls and I am very proud of that. Maybe as you say the collection established me somehow but to me a great part was about a bunch of clothes put together and that's part of the charm.

FM: How does the body affect the way you work on your collections?

OT: I wouldn't say that the body is my starting point but the body is inherent to all approaches I can have in designing clothes and therefore can be considered as a base, a foundation to my work. I often start drawing or thinking of a collection after I have defined a body canvas to draw on to but after a while I get rid of it and eventually disregard these initial tries. The body is something I very much like to look at, the variety of morphologies, I see it as very natural thing and I like my own body too... to touch the body, to work with the body, to observe it, form it. I am very happy when I can simply be on a beach, watching people walking by, look at them, their shape.

FM: With no intention to compare your collections at Rochas and Nina Ricci to what you are doing now, they both reflected much more ambition, sex, and fantasy at moments, while now you keep a more quiet tone. Yet, you are the same person and all of these approaches are your achievements but I do wonder about the shift from that version of Olivier Theyskens to what you are today. And where did the body stand then for you?

OT: The explanation is kind of simple because times have changed.

We are still working on excellent models as we did then; we are showing our clothes on amazing, uniquely beautiful and incredible girls, which can make even a simple dress look more interesting. I guess it's a nowadays thing to me to design in a "quieter way" probably because, frankly I do not feel so much excited these days with the idea of a girl getting to some degree of extravaganza. It feels a little bit dated, although I have always loved this kind of things but now I do not feel at all approaching fashion in such a way. While I am working I come across the simple question whether something is right or wrong to do and I choose to find "fantasy", as you say, wrong. You mentioned before the themes of a collection, the relation with the body is also that. I'm not sure it feels so modern to be a designer who underlines too much the concept that is connected to the body in terms of distortion or exaggeration. There is something that makes this feel uneasy and too much image-oriented which doesn't feel totally modern to me now.

FM: There was another collection where I thought you became over sexual, rough and edgy (Nina Ricci Autumn Winter 2009)! The clothes were very close and deforming the body, elongating the silhouette with very sharp edges; the body was not suffocated but it was rather introduced as something very powerful...

OT: Indeed that collection was deforming a lot, starting from the shoulder pads on the jackets, for example — instead of being placed on top of the shoulders they were drifted to the front of the outfit. They were literally pointing like four breasts on the front of the jacket and this made them appear very aggressive. There was a lot of distortion on each look, the body, the extension of the legs.

The intention was to be more cool, edgy and dark and at the same time to have this certain Serge Lutens magic, evening, sparkling and shining edge. The collection was drawn very fast, maybe in one or two days and the sketches — which were also on exhibit at the MoMu — were very discreet, they were very small, quick-made in pencil and they show just a profile... I mean these sketches suggested how the dresses would look without too much thinking or details. It was just about the allure of the girls and how they would walk. The adaptation of the silhouette was to make the girls look like these very quick-made sketches, which then became a very technical process in the making of the clothes.

On the contrary, the drawings from the collection just before were extremely worked and detailed; every bit of colour, material, shade was drawn in a very precise way. I think because the Nina Ricci 2009 Spring Summer collection was such a long and detailed process I later had a natural potency to go quick and fast with just a scribble sketch. This also reflected my own balance at the time. Sometimes I would go very soft and then be the exact opposite.

Recently I started drawing on an i-Pad Pro and finding all the practical advantages and the ways to use it to organise my materials. My sketches are now changing from collection to collection.

FM: Can we read humans through clothing?

OT: You can but you can also make great mistakes. There are methods that people use. When you look at Angela Merkel, she probably knows that her look is not super high fashion but she will be more loved by wearing more low-key clothes that keep her closer to the hearts of everyday people. Being too sophisticated would be politically very bad for her. So, in the end, you don't know what her real taste is. If you are in a city like New York, you can see girls that are pretty well dressed and you know it is a formality, that it's because of the way it goes there, how they shine next to their friends and it's somehow motivated and not necessarily connected to one's real identity.

This might sound strange, as I am a fashion designer, but I am very cautious not to look on how people are dressed. I am not really appreciative of fashion victims or people that are too much "fashion showy". Especially these couple of years there's a shift in how people dress and as time passes, I feel it was much cooler before, but at the same time it's wrong to be judgemental. It also depends on the feeling you have, how much you can sense about a person and character. It's dangerous to label people by the way they dress.

FM: How connected are fashion designers today to the body they design for? In the end, what does clothing serve today?

OT: Such great sum of fashion, the fact of being really authentic to the body and the creative process or the depth of making something; all these measures are not necessarily connected.

Nowadays' rolling system dictates that if you have an Instagram account, you post a green sweater today, tomorrow you post a purple pair of jeans or the day after you post a cocktail dress and you just keep people on their toes, surprised and busy with something that can be crap at the end of the day! What you achieve is getting their attention for a very short while. On the other side you can be a very focused person who does things step by step, always posting stories that look alike and at the end people are bored of you.

I would disconnect the reasons per se why some designers are paying attention to the body while others are only about being photogenic. My personal focus is the body but I try to be cautious, it's a sad fact that not many people today try on clothes and truly acknowledge the cut, the making and the work behind a garment, whether it functions in an interesting way on the body and whether it is a great design. I just think of how people are not always interacting with fashion the way they would do before — they no longer look at it the same way — therefore I am interested in always finding a way to keep me excited because I will not hesitate to make choices that I feel are the right ones. When it comes to what we were talking about, the proportion, the complexity of clothes, I can tell you, I had them in the hands during the mounting of my exhibition. I am completely aware of how they are made. I could draw things that are similar or at the same level, but I do not think it is the right thing to do right now. It's probably a condition because of the way fashion is digested and the way it happens to be today.

FM: Why do you think that there are more people interested in fashion than ever before?

OT: A lot of times I am thinking we are very much, and like never before, like an aquarium. In my career I took a sabbatical year three times, which of course sounds crazy but for me it was an important thing to do. Three times, I stepped out of the fashion world; each for a whole year and I became completely disconnected while looked at everything from afar. I think maybe in the eighties and nineties people would buy magazines to look at the outside world, they would watch TV, perhaps they would buy "Elle" magazine for example as it would give them back a precise message about the epoch they lived in. People were updated once a month from a few media sources and getting inspired by that. Now information comes from everywhere, we have so much to put our hands on and magazines perhaps are not as effective anymore.

In the end, my mother... I do not think she knows very much about what is going on and who is new or where. Particularly for designers who lived that media era and how that changed, like me let's say, it's nice to discover today that people knew us then without the social media we have now or without any of these new communication systems. We have to convert ourselves because nobody from the new generation will know us soon. I am very happy for my recent exhibition for example, because many of the visitors got to know my work and me accidentally.

EMOTION

FM: "She Walks in Beauty" was your retrospective exhibition, which was held at the MoMu in Antwerp and closed in March 2018. The title by itself is very emotional. I wonder if you were interested in observing how the audience perceives your work? In what ways and at what level?

OT: The title, which as you know, is connected to Lord Byron's poem, is rather less emotional as it is actually atmospheric as many of my shows

— not necessarily today, as my shows are not atmospheric or emotional anymore, yet they have been. In the exhibition it was very important for me to reflect that notion of the way I would present these shows, as they carry highly atmospheric moments, there would be some kind of a feeling that is almost like weather forecasting.

The thing about poetry is that it is always emotional but there is as well something very spacious about it, this is why I put poems in the exhibition, because they can reveal a more global feeling. They can speak about a concept or emotion without being explicit about it and touch many at the same time.

FM: I wonder about your feelings, when you walked around your exhibition at the MoMu...

OT: I loved and felt very proud of it but I also felt that I couldn't look at any of it without putting those clothes into the context of the time period they were made, the environment, the general fashion scene and this is my conclusion.

The language that has been articulating in the shows has always been a language within a moment, a situation, within something that had to be done at that given moment. Behind what might be stylish or just tasteful choice there's also the feeling I had whether something was useful to do or not.

For example, if I take the 2009 Spring Summer Ready-to-Wear collection for Nina Ricci, at the time it was extremely useful for the House to show its capacity in terms of atelier, because we had been working for two years to build a better team of hands and pushing the level higher in terms of craft, patternmaking and design. It was very important to show this shift and start a dialogue on that capacity because the House wasn't regarded as a Couture House, it was more of a straggling house at the time. My motivation was not just to make pretty dresses but also to show to the world that Nina Ricci had a capacity of action at the level of a great atelier. The collection that followed with the extremely high-heeled shoes was about that, but also for bringing an edge and a more contemporary ready-to-wear out.

FM: Were there certain pieces in the exhibition that have been carrying more emotions than others?

OT: There are, especially when they are connected to people I loved to work with. As a matter of fact I have been working on these collections at the time for being able to show them. The emotion would build up when the collection would bring it at the exact moment of the presentation. If I were to show them again in our present time, the pieces would be perhaps not as emotional as they were then, considering the girls that were wearing them, a certain environment or sound, the progression of the looks on the catwalk, watching the collection unfold silhouette after silhouette.

FM: So you can manoeuvre emotion through a show?

OT: I may have such intentions, and many times I would put together the line-up of all the looks on paper even before we'd start working on them to see if the collection can deliver. It's a bit like a movie script where you put together the story, create the characters, emphasise on them, you try some emotional picks here and there... so yes, I have tried to work in a similar manner. I would feel that this colour on this dress might cause a certain effect or that a specific model should definitely wear a certain look and so on. It was truly my intention to have a strong show that would as well be remembered for the emotions it would bring to the guests and journalists.

FM: Why is the ceremonial process of dressing linked with achieving a higher state of feelings?

OT: When you put together the right ingredients and they work in a show, the result is always mesmerising; and I am referring to the past, I am not talking about now — how we would have a great cast of models placed in the right setting, great music and story telling, we would suddenly hit a chord and make it happen. It would not work for every collection, as it is a magic and rare moment that has no real recipe. One of the reasons that I am no longer focused on such ways of presentation is because the notion of "magic" is slightly shuttered by the i-Phones, the attitude, it's something that happens on a global level and it's definitely a moment that does not fit such ways of expression. Maybe things will soon change again. When you think of past shows for example, Polly Mellen was there, Bill Cunningham was there, cell phones did not exist and the guests were looking at everything you wanted them to see. They would honour the reason they were invited at a show.

I remember vividly Marie-Christiane Marek when she was working at Paris Première TV channel and she came to do a live broadcasting of the show while she would simultaneously describe the looks as they were walking by. People sitting around would hate her for that because she would interfere with their focus on the collection.

Today you are literally sitting next to a person who is checking up emails, taking selfies, puts the phone in front of your face... There is no way you can try and carry this whole audience and bring them to a state of global emotion.

The approach and how people are committed today is completely different. It's not anymore about just a soul watching a show for which they are passionate about. Today it is about being constantly connected with the social media and the closer you are to something that is considered as hype, the higher your position is in terms of followership, likes, etc.

We are so far from the moment when people would fight to get inside an obscure show because they really wanted to see it. Today many people choose the shows they attend based on the fact that they want themselves to be seen and be photographed. Of course there are those who remain traditionally loyal to fashion but as a whole, this is no longer the focus.

This new digital era of fashion is also a bit funny and disconnected from other aspects of life.

FM: Why do we exhibit fashion in museums, apart from the financial and historical reasons?

OT: When MoMu contacted me for an exhibition on my work, I didn't fully understand what they were asking from me. I thought they just wanted me to curate something thematic, not something focused on my personal work.

While experiencing the retrospective I was impressed by the opportunities it could bring. An exhibition is a useful tool to perhaps refresh the memories. It also allows you to follow one's process. It offers the possibility to discover more. In my case, it is useful because some people and journalists today happen to think that my career actually started with Rochas and I would have to remind them that I did my own brand before for five years.

People tend to forget or have difficulty to accept things. If someone started their career later it's natural that what I've done earlier might be unknown to them, being one of the nineties–two thousands breed of designers. So it was a good choice to have this exhibition and to be able to show the different chapters of what I have done and still continue doing.

POLITICS

FM: How does the media serve you and how do you serve the media?

OT: When I started working I was very excited about everything from designing clothes, cut them, sew them sometimes, working with the craftsmen, the manufacturers and then I was delighted to give the collection to a press agency and the media to do their work. You wouldn't have to do anything; you just waited to see the result. Today it sounds so crazy to have to contribute and feed the people with a website, images, etc. As a designer I find it very hard as it's much more demanding now than it ever was.

I play the game but I never felt I signed for that.

Today it's also hard to measure how much of that demand is important or not. Considering that the magazines also have a problem now in general. Sometimes I want to scream "Who is reading this?" I actually want to meet the people who are excited to buy magazines and read them, I'm wondering who they are.

I do acknowledge that a part of who I am today is owed to how magazines, incredible photographers, stylists and models contributed to build my image as a designer. If this would be the same today it would make me really happy but there is a problem as the gaze of people on magazines has changed too. I wonder if they are looking at all. Would you even consider the moment that someone like Irving Penn would take that incredible picture and you putting it on Instagram the next minute?

It would never be right! You would first want to see it printed, give it the time and the respect it deserves. I hope I'm making sense. The media are extremely important for the brands and it helps so much that your name is introduced to a much broader audience, to globally validate you, they do serve so many important principles, making your brand more inclusive, it's true. But now magazines have a problem because this is a moment of change and perhaps we need to see clearer of what is coming.

It's like museum exhibitions. I was very lucky to have an exhibition but recently I was reading an article on it saying that many brands and marketing business are considering the option of an exhibition as a very important way to promote brands. An exhibition is most of the times on for months and can attract visitors on a daily basis, in many cases it's a word-of-mouth news, it puts you in some sort of institutionalised brand context.

Lydia Kamitsis, who was one of the curators of my exhibition, was saying that ten–fifteen years ago it was very difficult to convince anyone to give you clothes for an exhibition, designers would hate that and take it almost like an insult, especially those who were still active in fashion.

They would be scared to see themselves in a museum because to them it meant they were finished.

FM: What about the way fashion is formed today? Who is really directing it in your opinion?

OT: It depends on what you mean by "fashion". Everyone knows that there are people who are highly conditioned by the economical aspect of the fashion world and much of it is connected with the power that some groups have and the power that some individuals have gained in that world; which is activated by the people who are OK to support that.

To answer the question "who really rules the world", you can say of course the government or the lobby... True fashion is someone like you who is interested, who does exhibitions, you write about it and you question people, you take photographs while considering any potential designer as a source of interest and you dig even deeper for more information to share with others. You love what you do! Yet, many institutions do not think like this, they just don't apply this system as they are in another type of logic that is also conditioning much of the media today, because they just have to exist and they do not have much choice to exist and they have to bound and accept crazy conditions. They are less fashionable because they do not speak of personal choice, they do not speak of individual taste. They speak only through pseudo business-oriented relationships when in essence they are not excellent business minds.

When you are a fashion editor, you are not necessarily a good businessman.

I do not really see this as true fashion. Personally I feel like I understand the problem and its root and it globally touches many institutions in many fields the same way, but when it comes to fashion where people have to declare what they like, what they find beautiful and what they are excited by, you can see there are many conditions underneath. It makes me slightly smile sometimes.

FM: Not more than twenty years ago, designers such as McQueen and John Galliano were creating entire collections inspired by tribes, global historical references, and folklore. Today this approach is considered as inappropriate. What happened in between?

OT: The approach is different! Back then designers would get inspired and create; they would make their own clothes by all these references. They would rework ideas and make something incredible out of that. I question myself too, being a designer who creates collections based on themes and stories, building ideas around an artist, an era, a historical moment, etc. I just feel today this approach is perhaps not very cool or modern. This is why I now design my collections the way I do and it is there to question some of the situations that we are exposed to nowadays. I often follow my intuition and after all I start thinking the reasons. Not the other way round.

VIKTOR & ROLF

Fashion Artists

BODY

FILEP MOTWARY: How is the meaning of the "body" approached in fashion generally, how is it approached by V&R specifically, considering its permanent outline and the fact that it is something generic?

VIKTOR & ROLF: In our work the body serves as the carrier of the garment. We tend to think of clothes as sculptures or as props; as autonomous objects, or as pieces that play a part in a bigger story, i.e. the show. Of course clothes need to be wearable. But wearability is a relative concept.

FM: What about the technological body, the body that is dressed by computerised clothing? Why does the body still need to look and act human?

V&R: What comes to mind is this: every body is different. The average body does not exist. But ready-to-wear, and high street fashion (any fashion not just made to measure actually) are based on standardisation.

Size scales are based on averages. So there is a paradox in standardised fashionable clothes.

FM: How connected are fashion designers today to the body they design for?

V&R: As a designer the body is one of the basics to deal with.

FM: Why do body standards change over the years, while certain attributes remain as classics?

V&R: Changes in society, which cause the roles of the genders to change, are especially and clearly reflected in the changing lines of fashion. Certain areas of the body may be continuous points of focus; but their shape is fluid and will morph according to the latest fashion.

FM: What forces these changes in your opinion? From "The Birth of Venus" (c. 1486) by Botticelli, to Marie Antoinette, Louise Brooks, Bettie Page, Twiggy, Kim Kardashian...

V&R: Changes in society are reflected in fashion. Certain people may adopt these changing fashions sooner than others and become icons of the style of a certain era. The real change, unlike trends, is generated by the broader movements that come from within society itself. Personal style may fascinate an audience, but only if it resonates with a broader social context.

FM: At the end, what does clothing serve today?

V&R: The way fashion is consumed nowadays feels a bit like bulimia. If fashion equals food, what does that say about our society?

FM: Can we read humans through clothing?

V&R: An outfit is a signal.

FM: Humans have been working on reconstructing the body and proportion through clothing... Why this particular need?

V&R: It is always about power.

EMOTION

FM: Where in your opinion fashion meets with emotion?

V&R: The impulse to dress in a certain way is not rational to begin with. The size of the fashion business is the testament to the strength of the emotions that fuel this behaviour.

FM: Have you manoeuvred emotion through your fashion?

V&R: We use our work as a tool to convey emotions, most notably through the fashion show itself. By playing with the codes of the system, we have tried to express all kinds of emotions, from more sinister and dark (Black Hole; Atomic Bomb) to poetic and romantic (Silver; Vagabonds) to cerebral (Russian Doll), meditative (Zen Garden) or plain joyful and fun (Flowerbomb; Flowers).

FM: Why is the ceremonial process of dressing linked with achieving a higher state of feelings?

V&R: The act of putting on clothes in daily life is a bit like dressing for a play. Whether there is an audience or not is irrelevant. Getting dressed means getting ready for the role you are about to play in your life.

FM: Your work has been shared with the wider public, outside of the fashion show context on various occasions. Why do we exhibit fashion in museums today?

V&R: Next to our catwalk shows, we like to show our work in museums because it is such a democratic way of sharing it with a bigger audience. A fashion show is an exclusive affair for very few people, lasting a mere ten minutes. A museum show lasts longer and offers more control over the end product.

FM: Here I would like to focus on your Russian Doll collection (1999 Autumn WInter Haute Couture), which was very different in the way it was presented; it was an example of excellence, a demonstration of great artisanship and atelier skills. Yet today, perhaps it underlines as well our relationship with time, the importance of "gazing" at something as opposed to looking at it as well as a way of presenting fashion as work in process. Could you kindly elaborate? How long does it take for a model to be 100 per cent conscious of what she/he is wearing? How did Maggie Rizer reflect to her being the central model of that show at the time? Are you interested in the "self" of a model? How does your creative communication evolve?

V&R: Thank you. The Russian Doll show came about at a moment when we had very little money, so the decision to do a show with just one model was partly taken due to financial constraints. At the same time, our work often is a reflection on fashion itself. The idea to work with just one girl tied into our fascination with the fashion show as a ceremony. We conceived of the show as a performance, where every layer of clothing was put onto Maggie Rizer as if she were some kind of deity. Crystal embroidery on almost every layer served to accentuate a sense of extreme "richesse" [wealth] and the whole affair was meant to emphasise a sense of ritual, with beauty itself as an object of worship instead of a commodity.

FM: When is a garment, a look considered as iconic or emotional, based on your career? Where in your opinion fashion meets with emotion?

V&R: A look becomes iconic if it is often reproduced. It takes little time after a show to understand which looks people have the strongest reactions to. We turned this process of selection into a project: every season, the most iconic look of the show is recreated doll-size: we introduced these dolls at our retrospective at the Barbican in London in 2008, and have created an army of them ever since. Replicas of Victorian dolls showcasing the highlights of our career in miniature. It shows our fascination with time, and addresses the fleeting aspect of fashion. The dolls exist as a sort of souvenir, in order to cherish what we have done (instead of throwing it out at the end of the season). These mementos of the past, when put together, form a new work.

FM: Could we suggest clothing is a living organism?

V&R: Fashion certainly is, just look at the way it changes all the time.

POLITICS

FM: How would you describe the current state of fashion and why? What about the way fashion is formed today?

V&R: We don't really like to make general statements about fashion. As an industry it seems to be doing very well.

FM: Who is really directing it in your opinion?

V&R: The market.

FM: What is so important about being new? Does creation have to be new?

V&R: Originality and authenticity are very important to us, because we have always considered our work to be like a self-portrait. At the same time, very few things are really new.

FM: Would you agree that fashion, now more than ever before, has become self-referential, much more secluded and closed and entirely for those following fashion religiously?

V&R: Has that ever not been the case? At the same time, today these hermetic codes are copied by the high street and offered to a big audience!

FM: Is there room for fantasy today? How can we keep that doorway open for it?

V&R: Of course. People will always want to dream. It just seems that fashion is the catalyst for different things than dreaming at the moment.

FM: How does fashion serve liberty and vice versa?

V&R: Fashion makes you more aware of your individuality. An awareness of who you are leads to a consideration of your attitudes, responsibilities, duties and rights.

FM: The ways models present fashions on the catwalk changes every decade. Could you walk us through these changes and elaborate?

V&R: Roughly we have gone from the extreme posing (reminiscent of frozen fashion pictures) of say the fifties couture shows, to the more upbeat and theatrical mood of the seventies and eighties (where the actual showing of the clothes was turned into a spectacle) to a minimal, "neutral" way of moving. The role of photographers has changed entirely too: where at first they were banned altogether, in the seventies and eighties they did their work all around the catwalk, while today they are concentrated in the designated media area — with the audience collectively taking pictures at the same time as well. All of this influenced model's choreography and behaviour on the catwalk.

FM: We witness how a model's posture has changed, the use of hands, and the choreography that is now a rather straight walking line. How would you explain this phenomenon?

V&R: The way fashion is shown these days: fast; in straight lines; with models having little expression on their faces, combined with the ever shorter time span of shows suggest an over-all feeling of self-deprecating "efficiency". The implied message being that little time may be wasted.

FM: The word "intellectual" was coined at a time of extreme political anxiety. I wonder whether today, more than ever before, fashion has a political role? What are the needs covered through fashion?

V&R: We recently started emphasising what has been our credo from day one: that it is important for design to have a meaning. If there is no reason, why does it exist? We call it "conscious design": making something for a reason. "Reason" and "meaning" are not to be confused with "utility". Design can have a poetic reason of existence too.

ACKNOWLEDGEMENTS

Thank you Danilo Venturi for this wonderful opportunity to work with you. For your trust, encouragement and friendship!

Thank you Skira for publishing this book.

Thank you all the contributors and participants Hussein Chalayan, Jean Paul Gaultier, Pamela Golbin, Iris van Herpen, Harold Koda, Michèle Lamy, Thierry-Maxime Loriot, Antonio Mancinelli, Suzy Menkes, Violeta Sanchez, Valerie Steele, Jun Takahashi, Olivier Theyskens, Viktor & Rolf.

Thank you all at Polimoda: Candice-Reney Jooste, Gianpaolo D'Amico, Silvia Tolaro, Ornella Fazio, Georgina Riddiford, Eva Karhanova, Tessa Pisani, Gabriele Moschin and all at Villa Favard for your amazing help.

Thank you — without your help this project would not have been possible: Emma Sidibe, Florent Farinelli, Nicolas Delarue, Selim Chikh at Karla Otto, Nancy Chilton and Eugenia Santaella at The MET, Jelka Music at Jean Paul Gaultier, Emily Knight, Charlotte Knight, Britt Lloyd, Rob Rusling and Carrie Scott at SHOWstudio, Agnes Magoga and Sandro Ghiglione at Olivier Theyskens, Emma van de Merwe at Iris van Herpen, Gladys Rathod at Museum at FIT, Janet Fischgrund and Joanna Barrios at Rick Owens, Chieri Hazu at Undercover, Michèle Montagne.Paris, Michelle Ewin and Faye Ratliff at SPRING London, Stefania Daskalaki at Chalayan, Natasha Cowan at Condé Nast.

Thank you for your help, you are part of this book: Panayiota Panayi-Kouanta, Stella Moushioutta, Maria Kamberis, Loukia Tricha, Nicholas Georgiou.

Thank you Marco Vianello, Simona Scuri, Anna Albano, Emma Cavazzini at Skira and Laura Mirri at Open Lab.

BIOGRAPHIES

HUSSEIN CHALAYAN is known as fashion's storyteller, his multidisciplinary approach bridging the gap between design, art and technology. From his future-gazing garments that live outside trends to his thought-provoking and utterly unique pieces, Chalayan continues to offer the discerning consumer iconic collections.

His collections are known for innovative design, impeccable tailoring, drapery and an elegant minimalist aesthetic playing with the narratives constructed around culture and anthropology. He uses techniques that reference past skills and crafts combined with current technology whilst exploring shapes and details that critique fragmentations and dislocations in contemporary environments. Chalayan designs, promotes and sells Women's ready-to-wear, Pre and Show Collection, and Menswear.

Hussein Chalayan was born in 1970 in Cyprus's capital, Nicosia. He grew up in London and studied at London's Central Saint Martins College of Art and Design graduating in 1993 with his debut collection being purchased by iconic British retailer Browns. In 1994 he started his own label and his designs have influenced the face of fashion and art ever since. Throughout his career Chalayan has received global industry recognition.

He was nominated in 1995 for the Lloyds designer of the year award and was the winner of the first Absolut Creation Award. The following two years he was nominated for the Lloyds designer of the year award. In 1998 he was nominated for the Avant Garde designer at the VH1 Fashion Awards; in 1999 and 2000 he was nominated British Designer of the Year at the British Fashion Awards. This same year "Vogue" included him in a group of twelve designers set to change the face of fashion in the coming decade calling him the "premier intellectual designer of his generation".

In 2000 Chalayan was also named in "Time" magazine's list of the 100 most influential innovators of the twenty-first century and later as one of 100 all-time Fashion Icons. In 2002 he moved his internationally lauded fashion show from London to Paris where the collection is shown seasonally.

Since 2003 Chalayan has been using film to present some of the collections in narrative form as well as making art films and installations. His ideas often evolve around perception and the realities of modern life, with particular interest in cultural identity, migration, anthropology, technology and genetics.

Chalayan represented Turkey in the 2005 Venice Biennale with his film "Absent Presence" featuring actress Tilda Swinton who starred as a biologist analysing the neurosis and paranoia around terrorism through the use of genetic testing. As well as taking part in important exhibitions in the Victoria and Albert Museum in London, The Kyoto Costume Institute, The Metropolitan Museum of Art and MOMA in New York, Chalayan is one of the few designers who has had critically acclaimed solo exhibitions.

JEAN PAUL GAULTIER was born in 1952 in a Paris suburb and has started his career with Pierre Cardin in 1970, on the day of his 18th birthday. After working at Esterel, Patou and again at Cardin, Gaultier decided to start his own fashion house and staged his first show in Paris in 1976. Critical and commercial success followed quickly and by the early eighties he was one of the most talked about young designers.

From the beginning of his career, Jean Paul Gaultier wanted to show that beauty has many facets and that we can find it where we least expect it like in a lowly tin can which first became a bracelet and later the packaging for his hugely successful perfume. His menswear was launched in 1984 with the "Male Object" collection and in 1997 Gaultier has realised his dream of starting an haute couture collection, "Gaultier Paris". He was also the designer for Hermès womenswear from 2004 to 2011. Throughout his career Gaultier has worked in dance, music and cinema. His costumes for Madonna's Blond Ambition tour have left an indelible imprint on the popular culture. His first cinema costumes were for Peter Greenaway's "The Cook, The Thief, His Wife and Her Lover" in 1989. He also designed costumes for "The City of Lost Children" by Caro and Jeunet, "Fifth Element" by Luc Besson and has worked three times with Pedro Almodovar on "Kika", "Bad Education" and "The Skin I Live In".

PAMELA GOLBIN is an internationally renowned figure in the fashion industry, with extensive historical knowledge of cultural and design issues. She is a leading expert in contemporary fashion and has organised landmark exhibitions worldwide. Ms. Golbin is also a successful published author and is invited to lecture on a regular basis all over the world. Currently, Ms.

Golbin is Chief Curator of Fashion and Textiles at the Musée des Arts Décoratifs in the Louvre Palace in Paris. Since 1993, Ms. Golbin has organised over thirty exhibitions including major award retrospectives and has created benchmark projects such as the inaugural exhibition of the French year in China at the National Museum in Beijing. Ms. Golbin is the author of over a dozen respected books translated in several languages. Franco-Chilean born in Peru, Ms. Golbin was educated in New York's Columbia University and in Paris' La Sorbonne. She lectures at high profile institutions such as London's celebrated Royal College of Art, the Los Angeles County Museum of Art and the New York's Fashion Institute of Technology. She initiated the Annual Fashion Talks interviews in New York City bringing onto a public stage the most renowned names in contemporary fashion for one-on-one live discussion. As a radio producer, she has launched a series of French programmes analysing today's leading fashion designers. Pamela Golbin is also a frequent commentator on television in Europe and abroad as well as a regular contributor to art and fashion magazines.

IRIS VAN HERPEN is a Dutch fashion designer who is widely recognised as one of fashion's most talented and forward-thinking creators who continuously pushes the boundaries of fashion design. Since her first show in 2007 van Herpen has been preoccupied with inventing new forms and methods of sartorial expression by combining the most traditional and the most radical materials and garment construction methods into her unique aesthetic vision. She calls this design ethos "New Couture". Van Herpen is often hailed as a pioneer in utilizing 3D printing as a garment construction technique, and as an innovator who is comfortable with using technology as one of the guiding principles in her work because of its sculptural nature. The designer's intent is to blend the past and the future into a distinct version of the present by fusing technology and traditional couture craftsmanship. Her work has been featured in various museum exhibitions, including a major retrospective that is touring the United States since 2015, beginning with a six-month long run at the High Museum of Art in Atlanta. Six of her dresses were acquired by the Metropolitan Museum of Art in New York and seven of her works were exhibited in its highly successful 2016 "Manus x Machina: Fashion in an Age of Technology" show. In addition to the above, van Herpen's creations have been exhibited at the Victoria & Albert Museum in London, the Cooper Hewitt Museum in New York and the Palais de Tokyo in Paris, among others. Three solo books have been published on the designer's work — "Iris van Herpen" by the Groninger Museum to accompany her first solo exhibit, "Iris van Herpen: Transforming Fashion" by the High Museum of Art to accompany the United States museum tour, and most recently "Iris van Herpen Backstage". Van Herpen has received numerous awards since 2009. These include the Johannes Vermeer Award, state prize for the arts (2017), the ANDAM Grand Prix Award (2014) and the Grand Prize of the European commission – STARTS (2016).

The designer's interest in science and technology has led to ongoing conversations with CERN (The European Organization for Nuclear Research) and MIT (Massachusetts Institute of Technology). Today, van Herpen continues to work within her Amsterdam studio, where new ideas are born, and where Haute Couture orders are meticulously crafted for her global clientele, each creation passing through the designer's own hands.

HAROLD KODA, curator and author, is the former Curator in Charge of The Costume Institute at The Metropolitan Museum of Art. Since 1980, he has curated over fifty exhibitions primarily during his tenure at the Fashion Institute of Technology and The Costume Institute, but also at the Guggenheim Museum, The Bass Museum and other smaller galleries. He is the author and co-author of twenty books, and lectures widely. He initiated and orchestrated the transfer of the Brooklyn Museum's storied costume collection to the MET in 2009, and oversaw The Costume Institute's first major capital renovation in forty years, resulting in a state-of-the-art facility theatre opened as the Anna Wintour Costume Center in 2014. Born in Honolulu, he graduated from the University of Hawaii with a dual B.A./B.F.A. in English Literature and Art History, received an M.L.A. in Landscape Architecture from Harvard, and was the recipient of Honorary Doctorates from the University of the Arts London in 2014 and Drexel University in 2016. For his contributions to the field of Costume Studies, he has been honoured with awards from the Council of Fashion Designer's of America, the Fashion Group International, Pratt Institute, and Bard College among others.

MICHÈLE LAMY was born in Jura in 1944. She is an entrepreneur, collaborator, producer, wife and business partner to Rick Owens.

During the sixties and seventies she worked in Paris as a defence attorney. In 1979 she moved to Los Angeles where she created a clothing line, Lamy, and opened two landmark restaurants in Hollywood (Café des Artistes and Les Deux Cafés). In 2003 Lamy and Owens moved to Paris, and since then have been building their now widely celebrated world.

Within Owenscorp, Lamy functions as an instigator and all round special projects director. She works closely with the artisans in constructing the furniture as well as on Maison Objets (homeware) and HUNROD, her collaboration with jewellery designer Loree Rodkin.

Her personal projects, many of which focus on gathering and "feeding" a specifically curated audience in a "barge" environment to coincide with art fair moments, fall under the banner of Lamyland. In 2016 Lamy formed the conceptual band Lavascar with the sound performance artist Nico Vascellari and her artist daughter Scarlett Rouge.

They recorded the album "Montage of a Dream Deferred" as part of the Red Bull Music Festival in Paris, September 2016. From January–March 2018, Lamy was the first creative to be invited by Selfridges to take residency in their Corner Shop (Lamyland X Selfridges).

THIERRY-MAXIME LORIOT was born in Quebec City in 1976. He curated the various renditions of the globally successful touring exhibition "The Fashion World of Jean Paul Gaultier: From the Sidewalk to the Catwalk". Initiated by Nathalie Bondil, Director and Chief Curator of the MMFA, the retrospective travelled to twelve cities and drew more than two million visitors, breaking records for a fashion exhibition. Opened in Montreal in 2011, the exhibition travelled to Dallas (Dallas Museum of Art), San Francisco (Fine Arts Museums of San Francisco), Madrid (Fundación MAPFRE), Rotterdam (Kunsthal), Stockholm (Swedish Centre for Architecture and Design), Brooklyn (Brooklyn Museum), London (Barbican Centre), Melbourne (National Gallery of Victoria), Paris (Grand Palais), Munich (Kunsthalle der Hypo-Kulturstiftung) and Seoul (Dongdaemun Design Plaza), where the exhibition tour came to a close in June 2016. Loriot also co-curated the exhibition "Be My Guest" at the London College of Fashion (LCF) in 2014, and collaborated with Dr. Valerie Steele on the "Fashion Underground: The World of Susanne Bartsch" retrospective presented at the Fashion Institute of Technology (FIT) in New York in 2015.

Loriot's Jean Paul Gaultier world tour was followed by his exhibition "Love is Love: Wedding Bliss for All à la Jean Paul Gaultier", presented at the MMFA and at the Centro Cultural Kirchner in Buenos Aires. He also curated the travelling exhibitions "Peter Lindbergh: A Different Vision on Fashion Photography", and "Viktor & Rolf: Fashion Artists", first presented at the National Gallery of Victoria in Melbourne in 2016, followed by its presentation in the summer of 2018 at the Kunsthal Rotterdam in the Netherlands to mark the twenty-fifth anniversary of the pair. Loriot is also Consulting Curator for Fashion and Textiles at the National Gallery of Victoria in Melbourne, and at the Montreal Museum of Fine Arts in Canada. He is working on the first Thierry Mugler retrospective to open at Montreal Museum of Fine Arts in Winter 2019.

ANTONIO MANCINELLI is the Deputy Editor of the Italian Edition of "Marie Claire" since 2005. He began his career very early, at 19. He wrote a number of essays for the catalogues of major fashion exhibitions, the latest being for the retrospective exhibition for Rick Owens "Subhuman, Inhuman, Superhuman" at La Triennale di Milano presented by Eleonora Fiorani (2017), "Haute-à-Porter" by Filep Motwary (2016), "Italiana - L'Italia vista dalla moda 1971–2001", at the Palazzo Reale in Milan and published some books, including "Moda!" (2006), the monography "Antonio Marras" (2006) and "Fashion: Box", translated into many languages

(Japanese, too!). Since 1985 he has been teaching journalism, fashion journalism, and "Analysis of Fashion System" in different schools and universities in Italy and Europe: Bocconi University, Istituto Marangoni, Domus Academy, Istituto Europeo di Design, Politecnico, in Milan, "La Sapienza" in Rome, Alma Studiorum in Bologna, IUAV University in Venice, Polimoda in Florence.

He works as an author and hosts radio shows while he's regularly invited to tv shows in Italy. Besides "Marie Claire", he wrote for "Diario", "Vogue" Italia, "Elle", "Max", "Maxim", "Gioia", "Another Magazine", "Vanity Fair" Italia. He has a blog, he doesn't like "fashion people", he never missed an opening at La Biennale di Venezia and he feels to live like in a "complicated" relationship with fashion: but they love each other for sure. The second love of his life is milk chocolate. In another life he would have been a movie director. Or an actor. Now he is too old to choose.

SUZY MENKES is fashion's leading authority. As International "Vogue" Editor, her articles and reports appear on 21 international "Vogue" websites in 16 languages, reaching an audience of over 67 million. An enthusiast for social media, she has over 383,000 followers on Instagram.

Frank, fearless and free from editorial constraints, she has built a reputation for having a strong and independent point of view. She brings to her worldwide audience a deep knowledge, experience and love of fashion.

With an unswerving enthusiasm for her subject, she covers the universe of style, from haute couture to talent spotting and store openings, including both womenswear and menswear. She regularly interviews leading designers and fashion executives in the luxury market.

Unique among fashion editors, Suzy — trained as a historian at Cambridge University in her native England — looks beyond the immediate trends to analyse changing style in a social context.

Her incisive reporting includes financial news and reviews of museum exhibitions and the arts.

The luxury conference concept, which Suzy invented over a decade ago, while Fashion Editor of the "International Herald Tribune", shows a breadth of vision and geographical reach which can only be deepened as she now hosts conferences for Condé Nast International.

Suzy is a member of the French National Order of the Legion of Honor, where she holds the rank of Chevalier, and of the Order of the British Empire for "services to fashion journalism."

In 2013, she was awarded the Fiorino d'Oro — the highest honour of the city of Florence — in recognition of her contribution to culture and arts in that city. Later that year, she received a Special Recognition Award at the British Fashion Awards.

In 2014, she was honoured with a Lifetime Achievement Award by CEW — Cosmetic Executive Women.

In 2015 Suzy received the keys to the city of Florence from Mayor Dario Nardella, while hosting the first Condé Nast International Luxury Conference in the Palazzo Vecchio.

In 2016, Suzy was awarded honorary citizenship of the city of Seoul from Mayor Park Won-Soon, while hosting the second edition of the Condé Nast International Luxury Conference.

VIOLETA SANCHEZ began her career as a model in the early eighties, while performing at the theatre in a play auspiciously named "Succès". The set and costumes were designed by Paloma Picasso while the première was a very Parisian event...

A movie buff and fan of Marlene Dietrich's wardrobe, she wore for the occasion a smoking that was made-to-measure by a man's tailor in Paris, and sat at dinner next to a very nice older gentleman, with whom she got on famously. He told her he was a photographer, and asked if she would pose for him. His name was Helmut Newton.

A couple of weeks later someone called the theatre on behalf of Monsieur Yves Saint Laurent, who was also in the audience on the night of the première, to propose her to "pose" for his next Haute Couture show. As they say, the rest is history.

She continues performing to this day in theatre, cinema and contemporary art pieces while pursuing a career as a model, for Yves Saint Laurent, Thierry Mugler, Jean Paul Gaultier, Givenchy, Claude Montana, Franco Moschino, Versace, Valentino, Helmut Newton, Guy Bourdin, Antonio Lopez, Tony Viramontes, to name a few, and David Seidner whose exhibition she curated at the Pierre Bergé Yves Saint Laurent Foundation in 2008. She has been performing with Olivier Saillard for the past ten years. As a researcher she collaborated on various books for the publishing company Les Éditions du Regard.

VALERIE STEELE is director and chief curator of The Museum at the Fashion Institute of Technology, where she has organised more than twenty-five exhibitions since 1997, including "The Corset", "London Fashion", "Gothic: Dark Glamour", "Daphne Guinness, A Queer History of Fashion", "Dance and Fashion and Proust's Muse". She is also the author or editor of more than twenty-five books, including "Paris Fashion", "Women of Fashion", "Fetish: Fashion", "Sex and Power", "The Corset", "The Berg Companion to Fashion", and "Fashion Designers A-Z: The Collection of The Museum at FIT". Her books have been translated into Chinese, French, German, Italian, Portuguese, and Russian. In addition, she is founder and editor in chief of "Fashion Theory: The Journal of Dress, Body & Culture", the first peer-reviewed, scholarly journal in Fashion Studies. Steele combines serious scholarship (and a Yale Ph.D.) with the rare ability to communicate with general audiences. As author, curator, editor, and public intellectual, Valerie Steele has been instrumental in creating the modern field of fashion studies and in raising awareness of the cultural significance of fashion. She has appeared on many television programs, including The Oprah Winfrey Show and Undressed: The Story of Fashion. Described in "The Washington Post" as one of "fashion's brainiest women" and by Suzy Menkes as "The Freud of Fashion", she was listed as one of "The People Shaping the Global Fashion Industry" in the Business of Fashion 500 (2014–present).

JUN TAKAHASHI was born in 1969 in Kiryū, Gunma Prefecture, Japan. He founded Undercover in 1990 with his friend Nigo while they were still at the Bunka Academy of Fashion. Soon after, he presented his first collection in 1994, during Tokyo fashion week. In 2002 he made his debut on the Paris catwalks for the 2003 Spring Summer season. In 2010, in collaboration with Nike, he launched a performance running collection called Gyakusou. In 2015, he curated the brand's first museum exhibition "Labyrinth of Undercover: 25 Year retrospective" which was held at the Tokyo Opera City Art Gallery. In 2018 he was invited at Pitti Immagine Uomo as a Guest Designer for the second time and held a show for 2018 A/W men's collection with Takahiromiyashita TheSoloist.

OLIVIER THEYSKENS made his debut in Belgium in 1997, when he presented his first collection of feminine, high-fashion, women's ready-to-wear. He then decided to show his following collection in Paris during the Fashion week and rapidly found international distribution and expansive editorial coverage. "Voguerunway.com" characterises his early work as consisting of "strong, dark collections that electrified fashion in the late nineties." In 2002, Theyskens moved to Paris when he was appointed artistic director of Rochas, a position he held for four years.

For his work at Rochas he was awarded the Star Award from Fashion Group International in 2005 and the title of Best International Designer by the CFDA in 2006. That same year, Theyskens took over the position of artistic director at Nina Ricci, where he infused the house with what Women's Wear Daily described as "his, strong suit […] stunning evening dresses that are soft and fluid". Theyskens' unique aesthetic was captured in a personal book project, "The Other Side of the Picture" (Assouline, 2009). The book is an anthology of images that offer an intimate insight into Theyskens' work throughout the years. In 2010, Theyskens joined contemporary fashion brand Theory to create Theyskens' Theory. In November of that year, Theyskens was appointed artistic director of the global Theory brand, where he stayed until 2014. In 2016, he made his re-entry on the Paris stage with his own eponymous label for Spring Summer 2017.

After his tenures in both European and American fashion houses, a contemporary vision of his own DNA resurfaces: little black leather dresses framed with lace, tartan coats, bustier tops, bias-cut gowns, and the ever-present hook-and-eye closures on shoes, shirts and jackets. Distributed internationally in top tier stores, the Olivier Theyskens brand has secured after three seasons its unequivocal position as a recognised twenty-first century luxury ready-to-wear Maison. In October 2017 the Antwerp fashion museum, MoMu, unveiled "Olivier Theyskens - She Walks in Beauty", a comprehensive retrospective covering twenty years of the designer's career thus far. Throughout his career, Olivier Theyskens has also collaborated with different artists, creating costumes for the Chicago-based rock band The Smashing Pumpkins, for the Théâtre de la Monnaie in Brussels and for the New York City Ballet, as well as creating special dresses for major celebrities and prominent socialites.

VIKTOR & ROLF is the avant-garde luxury fashion house founded in 1993 by fashion artists Viktor Horsting and Rolf Snoeren after their graduation from the Arnhem Academy of Art and Design. Widely recognised and respected for its provocative Haute Couture and conceptual glamour, the house of Viktor & Rolf aspires to create spectacular beauty and unexpected elegance through an unconventional approach to fashion.

Staging signature collections for over twenty years during Paris Fashion Week — ever since the first Haute Couture collection in Spring Summer 1998 — Viktor & Rolf creations evoke a provocative spirit infused with surreal contrasts. With Mariage and Soir, Viktor & Rolf presents its luxury bridal and eveningwear collections — an exploration of iconic elements inspired by classic couture influences. Viktor & Rolf's luxury products include exclusive eyewear line Viktor & Rolf's Vision, and an addictive catalogue of fragrances featuring worldwide bestsellers: Flowerbomb, Spicebomb, Bonbon and Magic.